MW00625978

Control in Conflict

254
WAL

FIRST BAPTIST CHURCH LIBRARY
16TH & "O" STS., N.W.
WASHINGTON, D.C. 20036

CONTROL IN CONFLICT

John Wallace

BROADMAN PRESS
NASHVILLE, TENNESSEE

© Copyright 1982 • Broadman Press

All rights reserved

4230-01

ISBN: 0-8054-3001-6

Unless otherwise noted, all Scripture quotations are taken from the King James Version of the Bible.

Scripture quotations marked GNB are taken from the *Good News Bible*, the Bible in Today's English Version. Old Testament: Copyright © American Bible Society 1976; New Testament: Copyright © American Bible Society 1966, 1971, 1976. Used by permission.

Scripture quotations marked NIV are taken from the HOLY BIBLE *New International Version*, copyright © 1978, New York Bible Society. Used by permission.

Dewey Decimal Classification: 254

Subject Headings: CHURCH WORK // CHURCH FELLOWSHIP

Library of Congress Catalog Card Number: 82-72227

Printed in the United States of America

To the Memory of My Father
John T. Wallace

FOREWORD

When he went through a Personal and Professional Growth Course, John Wallace was affectionately dubbed the "gunslinger." We all were impressed by his western pioneer mind-set to get to the bottom of things. He has the rare ability to combine candor and warmth when he confronts. He is fearless. But he is diplomatic. He is much more like the gunslinger Matt Dillon than he is the gunslinger Billy the Kid. Like Matt, he is concerned with justice and compassion. Unlike Billy the Kid, he would never shoot without reason (figuratively, not literally). He is not afraid of conflict. But he does not bring it on needlessly.

I have long felt that John Wallace was full of creativity that needed a vent. The appropriate vent is in this book he has written out of his long, enduring, and profitable experience.

The endearing part of the way John Wallace deals with conflict is that it is unmistakably Christian. It is the biblical manner of finding how conflict can be resolved with redemption that intrigues the reader. The reader will find much of that manner reflected by the way Jesus related to conflict situations.

When John first developed his idea about control in conflict, he was encouraged to write from his own experience rather than develop a rather lofty treatise. The statements or treatises have already been developed. John has written from his experience. He has witnessed many of the situations he has written about. He has worked through the conflict. He is a pilgrim who has made his way.

The statement made by John in this book needs to be said. It could not have been said earlier because the time was not right. Now the time is right.

BROOKS R. FAULKNER

INTRODUCTION

When I told some friends I was writing a book about conflict, they were puzzled. "Why are you writing on such an unpleasant subject? No one likes conflict, especially in the church."

We may not like it, but life is permeated with conflict. Most of the subjects on which we write involve conflict; even the favorite theme of love is interwoven with strife. Controversy is also a serious problem within the church.

The Bible teaches that we are to "follow after the things which make for peace, . . . that there be no divisions among you; but that ye be perfectly joined together in the same mind and in the same judgment. . . . Endeavouring to keep the unity of the Spirit in the bonds of peace. . . . And be at peace among yourselves" (Rom. 14:19; 1 Cor. 1:10; Eph. 4:3; 1 Thess. 5:13). Many other Scriptures emphasize that we are responsible for controlling conflict and living peaceably. But we blunder when caught in controversy. We lack the skills to control ourselves and resolve our differences with Christian grace.

Some church members think it is their privilege to be contentious. Some believe they have a right to fight in their church. Unfortunately, many people do not know any other way to handle controversy than in a belligerent manner.

My earliest memories of church are very dear to me. But those memories also hold scenes of strife that pain me to this day. In my Christian pilgrimage I have experienced the joys of relationship in several churches. I love the church, but I see a grievous weakness in the way we resolve our differences. We can improve if we work to develop control in conflict. Today there is an awareness of the need to develop conflict resolution skills among pastors and congregations. I would add my testimony to this emerging knowledge. This book contains stories of my pilgrimage and some lessons I've learned through conflict. The names I use are fictional to avoid any hint of identity.

Although I've studied scores of books on the subject, this is not a scholarly treatment of theories and technicalities in conflict management. I've tried to do as Brooks Faulkner suggested and write from my experience rather than research. Brooks is a supervisor at the Sunday School Board of the Southern Baptist Convention.

When I came to this church thirty-three years ago it was the Felix Memorial Baptist Church. But in 1964 we moved tne congregation and changed the name of the church. This book may give the wrong impression that we've been fighting all this time. To the contrary, we've lived in peace and love most of those years. If our people were not patient and loving, neither they nor I would be in that church today. When I was a seminary student a professor told our class that if we stayed with a church, we would likely have a major crisis about every seven years. We've not had that many. There have been only three major conflicts during these years. Of course, there have been the normal differences people experience when they work together.

A word of appreciation is due some special people who have helped me with this book. My family has been a wonderful support all through the years. Mary is a wise and loving wife; she has been God's best help to me in all our trials. My children, John, James, and Fern, have endured their daddy's frustrations behind the closed doors of home. That each of them is an active, adult Christian is a testimony to their individual faith and love in the Lord Jesus.

Some friends gave me inestimable help when I began the struggle of writing this book. Thanks to Charlie Shedd for his constructive encouragement in my writing. Brooks Faulkner urged me to write from this intensely personal approach. Bob Humphreys was a friend and counselor during some difficult days. Pastor Roger Lovett lifted my spirit when I verged on giving up this writing. To the dear people of my church who have strengthened my life in the conflicts of ministry, I am ever grateful.

JOHN WALLACE

Lexington, Kentucky
May 1982

CONTENTS

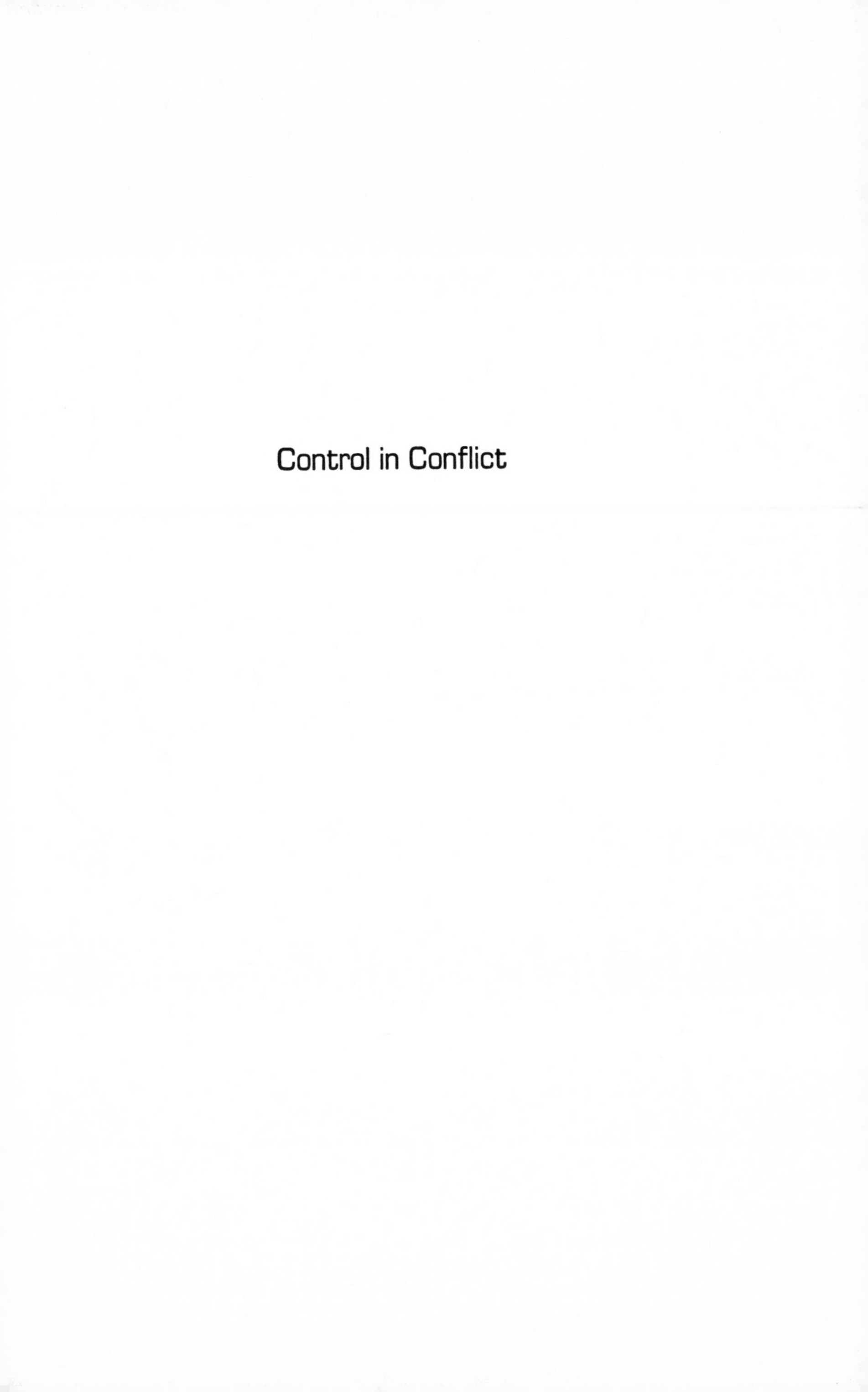

Control in Conflict

1

The Inevitable Crisis

The spring of 1968 saw Columbia University under physical assault from protesting students. Vietnam War opponents took occupancy of buildings on Columbia's campus. Dialogue between the administration and rebelling students was fruitless. Finally, police were called in to evict S.D.S. from the buildings.

Overlooking College Walk is the placid statue of *Alma Mater.* On the morning of April 30 she sat immobile before a turbulent sea of students. About her bronze neck hung a crudely lettered sign: "Raped by the cops." The school was humiliated by this incident. But not by the cops! This debacle wasn't the result of police intervention. Violence flared because those in disagreement failed at reasonable communication.

There is a subtle parallel to this incident with *Alma Mater.* Another feminine symbol, the church, might have a sign hung over her: "Abused by conflict." Church members disagree; but rather than patiently work out their problems, they often express hostilities which hinder and disrupt the work of the church.

Controversy is inevitable in the church, as on a college campus. Differences occur among people, but crises develop when persons do not resolve their disagreements peaceably.

There are two conspicuous approaches to variance in the church: either ignore the problem and hope it will fade, or take sides in a hostile contest. Emotion then becomes the determining factor in a win/lose struggle among the members.

My first awareness of controversy among Christians came when I was a boy. My family was active in a small-town church where fights broke out often. Since then I've noticed little change in the way conflict is handled in other churches. Programs of Christian ministry are different today, but few congregations have innovated strategies for resolving disagreements. The win/lose plan is still the only way most churches have of settling disputes. A new perspective toward settling differences is urgently needed.

Harmony among church members is a New Testament ideal. But our humanity makes conflict an inevitable experience. Even Jesus recognized there would be alienating differences among his followers. In the only places recorded where our Lord mentioned the church by name, conflict is present. Matthew 16:18 quotes Jesus: "Upon this rock I will build my church; and the gates of hell shall not prevail against it." No matter how you interpret "the gates of hell," the church is obviously involved in struggle. In Matthew 18:15, Christ tells how offended believers should behave. He was sensitive to the reality that not only in the world will we have tribulation, but at church we will have trouble.

Much of Paul's writings deals with disagreement among Christians. But we've largely ignored Paul's counsel. We proclaim the Bible as our guide "in faith and practice." But we believe only what we want and practice only what is convenient.

When conflict arises, a major hindrance is the reluctance to admit a problem. Too often our attitude is, *Just don't discuss it; it'll go away.* Sometimes I'm tempted to heed advice given me when I was a rural pastor. A farmer counseled me about discord in our church. "Preacher, just walk around it, step over it, don't try to move it, and you won't stir up any stink." Such advice sometimes leaves unpleasant consequences, both in the church and barnyard.

After seminary I became pastor of a church in a small southwestern town. That spring I married. My bride and I moved our scant belongings into an ancient parsonage. We gilded our poverty with love and began our ministry for Christ.

Soon afterward I learned that this church had a startling omission. Although it had a congregational form of government, the members never met in business session. Reports of church activities were never made, and decisions about needs were not voiced. Even the finances of the church were ignored. The money was handled by Clint, the church treasurer. He picked up the offerings, paid the bills, but gave no report to the people. I asked several members about their lack of participation in the church business. Answers were tactfully evasive.

After I began questioning the business procedures, a former pastor knocked at my door. I invited Reverend Dumpty in, but he preferred to stand on the porch. He chatted aimlessly, then spoke abruptly.

"John, I was here long enough to know that this is a good place to be *from*. If I were you, I wouldn't stay here any longer than it takes to find another church. You can't change this situation, so don't try! If you want to do anything differently, ask Clint. If you see a hard glint in his eye, forget it! Now I've got to go. God bless you, son." With that he left.

After Reverend Dumpty's visit, every time I went to Clint he had a hard look in his eye. So I did not go back to him when I considered renovating the church basement. Little children met there for Sunday School. It was a depressing place. Their early impressions of the "house of God" were gotten in that drab room. So, instead of asking Clint, I suggested remodeling the room to the ladies who taught there. They were delighted.

Clint learned of this idea and told me the work could not be done because the church didn't have the money. "Besides," he warned, "if the church did have the money, I wouldn't spend it fixing up that basement; so don't make any bills. I won't pay them." He was the church treasurer; we were blocked.

It became obvious that the key to change was the power of decision. But how does change begin when nobody will confront the person who makes all decisions? People must be drawn into the process of deciding. However, I wondered if the people *wanted* a part in planning and decision making. The elected church workers were the logical ones to express a first opinion. So I announced a meeting of all elected leaders in the church. The purpose was to discuss procedures for making future plans of church activities. If they did not want to participate, I'd find out.

The morning after the announcement, I got one opinion. A phone call came from Bart, a prominent rancher. He called me to his office, a few blocks from my home. When I walked in, there were two other wealthy members of the church, Vic and Clint. Bart got right to the point without any friendly preliminaries.

"Brother Wallace, we felt you'd make us a good little preacher when we called you. But here you are, stirring up trouble! Now we don't want a fuss in our church."

"I don't want any trouble in the church. What are you talking about?"

"You know what he's talking about," growled Clint. "It's that meeting you called to whip up the people. It'll be a bigger fracas than you can handle."

"I don't plan to whip up anyone. I just want to find out what the church wants to do."

Bart leaned forward on his elbow and pointed a pistollike finger at me. "Now, preacher, go on back home, phone those people, and call off that meeting. We'll let you know what the church wants to do. You behave yourself, and we'll get along together." Bart paused, then threw the knockout punch. "If you don't, we three will withdraw all of our support, and the church will fold. Now you git!" he concluded with a whiplike flick of his finger. I looked at each one, saw no change in their faces, turned silently, and walked out.

Head down, I moved inexorably into the crisis of my decision. Fear cried out in my mind: *It's not Christian to have trouble in the church. God's people should love each other. You're about to strike out your first time at bat. Why jeopardize* your *future because of* these *people? It won't make any difference with them, so why bother?*

All of my high anticipation for ministry collapsed beneath the pressure forced upon me. I was afraid. I plodded home, closed the door, and dropped to my knees on the bare floor. My posture was not so much one of prayer as of pain in my knotted stomach. I stayed there, forehead on the rough boards, until my spirit calmed. I tried to pray, but words didn't make much sense. Then to my mind came a Scripture: "Know ye not, that to whom ye yield yourselves servants to obey, his servants ye are to whom ye obey" (Rom. 6:16). That settled it; I decided to go ahead with the meeting.

Most church leaders came to the meeting. Obvious exceptions were Bart, Vic, and Clint. However, Clint sent a note saying he was against the meeting. He did not attend because he had laryngitis and couldn't even whisper. Each person was asked to express how he or she would like to see the church develop. Everybody, except one man, spoke positively. When the meeting adjourned there was a new spirit of enthusiasm among our people.

In the days that followed there were discouragements. However, attendance grew, offerings increased, and the members were happy. When Bart and Vic saw this response they returned, supported the work, and were my friends. Only Clint was implacable.

It is obvious that our actions are influenced by past experiences. My early church life was dominated by two attitudes toward conflict. They were opposite postures which forced me into a painful ambivalence for many years. Experience finally taught me there are better ways to resolve controversy than either of these two.

"Peace at any price" was the first stance toward dissension I learned in church. The people who modeled this posture believed that prevailing peace is essential. However, I've learned that peace is not the crowning achievement of a church; righteousness is. Righteousness produces peace. "The fruit of righteousness will be peace;/the effect of righteousness will be quietness and confidence forever" (Isa. 32:17, NIV).

Redemptively we are declared righteous through faith in Jesus and so have peace with God. Ideally, the church is under the control of God's spirit, living righteously in peace. But practically, when we live righteously we do not always have peace with everyone. Sometimes we have a fight on our hands. Hopefully, right emerges from the conflict and true peace prevails.

Sometimes after controversy the calm that emerges is misinterpreted. There is quietness rather than clamor; disputes have ceased, but harmony is absent. This quietness is not the result of relationships within the church being right. Rather, it is the outcome of a philosophy of "let's have peace, no matter what." But those who advocate "peace at any price" do not plan to pay; they expect someone else to make the sacrifice. Such a peace always costs a great deal.

There was a second extreme position which influenced my early responses to conflict. It was the belief, *Controversy is a spiritual activity.* Such a view is often held by preachers. The favorite verse of Scripture for these zealots is Jude 3, "Ye should earnestly contend for the faith." Such folk are very contentious.

I knew such a belligerent person long ago. He was known as "the fightin'est preacher in Texas." This pastor seemed happiest when he was vilifying somebody. He was often accused of causing congregations to split. To this he replied: "Don't worry about Baptists fighting. We are just like a bunch of cats on an alley fence at night. It's fuss and split, fight and scratch—and what do you get? More cats! So let the churches fight and split—what do you get? More Baptists!"

At the time, that retort seemed both funny and valid. I have since learned that a finer cat comes from selective breeding than from brawling in an alley. So it is with churches; a legitimate church is formed by a fulfillment of the Christian mission rather than a back-alley fight.

Paul wrote to the church at Rome: "As much as lieth in you, live peaceably with all men" (Rom. 12:18). *The church must find ways to be at peace, not excuses to fight.* Paul did not advocate peace at any price; neither did he condone the belligerent spirit. Instead, he taught the congregations to oppose evil while maintaining peace among themselves.

The church is called to seek peace while facing confrontations. Yet few congregations consider how this may be done. Little study is made of ways to manage conflict within a fellowship. We ignore the guile of our humanity until we disagree. Then we forget the commands of God and resist his Spirit within us.

This book is written as a simple introduction to dealing with conflict in the local church. I hope it will encourage Christians to face and solve their differences constructively. Handling controversy effectively can be done, but it must be learned. Solutions to strife don't just happen. Maintaining peace is a learned discipline to which all Christians are called (Mark 9:50; Rom. 14:19; 2 Cor. 13:11; Heb. 12:14; 1 Pet. 3:8,12).

I write from a pastor's viewpoint. I realize there are other approaches to confronting conflict. There certainly is the large perspective from the congregation. Also, in many churches, solutions must include the professional staff members.

My position is in a moderate-sized church—five hundred resident members. I realize that large churches have their unique tensions, but small ones seem to fight more frequently. Big churches, like great ships, weather storms with less attrition than smaller congregations. What Saul Bellow wrote about modern Israel in his book *To Jerusalem and Back* may be applied to us. Bellow explained, "The weaker you are, the more conspicuous your offenses; the more precarious your condition, the more hostile criticism you must expect."[1] I can identify with that! Of course members in larger congregations also strive with opposition. But for those who struggle in small churches, their resources are weaker and their reassurances fewer.

2

A Tolerance for Error

A mile from our church an IBM factory makes electric typewriters. There are 2,500 parts in an IBM typewriter. Prodigious effort goes into fitting all these pieces into a superb machine. But making a fine typewriter involves more than the mechanics of production.

One key factor in quality production is a worker's attitude toward his task. When efficiency dropped on an assembly line, a manager learned that his skilled mechanics were aggravated with faulty parts. They wanted perfect components. Detecting flaws, adjusting, or discarding pieces reduced their production rate. Moods of anger and frustration were evident among workers.

A friend of mine who works at IBM was assigned to improve these conditions on assembly lines. He began by working with the operators. The problem was seen first in people rather than machines. Lectures were given where operators were told, "Although there is an ideal quality for each typewriter part, certain deviations from perfection are allowed." The talks pointed out, "In manufacturing there is a 'law of probability' that a certain percent of parts will be faulty. Obviously every item can't be perfect." Workers were taught how to change their attitudes toward flaws and still produce quality machines. They were encouraged to develop a "tolerance for error." They responded, dispositions improved, and production rose.

The church needs to develop its own tolerance for error. We must allow for human imperfection in our relationships. Everyone has flaws. But our impatience toward another's weakness sometimes sparks conflict. In theory we admit "no one is perfect," but in practice we act as though the other person should be. The tolerance for error we reserve for ourselves.

In human behavior there is a law of probability: With any extended human relationship, irritable differences will arise. Although 2,500 typewriter parts are a lot of pieces to work together, consider a church family working together harmoniously. Early in my ministry I puzzled at the difficulty of getting even a small group to cooperate. Just about the time I thought everyone was pulling together, they'd split and bunch up.

Then I learned a formula showing the possibilities of different relationships within a group. It is the number of people in a group times that number, minus one. Among six people: $6 \times 5 = 30$. Within a committee of six people there are thirty different possible relationships. Add to that the unknown attitudes within each person.

When we see matters from this perspective, we recognize that we need new ways of handling differences in the church. Thus conflict, though not avoided, may be managed.

The IBM approach to solving employee discontent with faulty parts began by changing attitudes. So the church must study how to alter opinions about controversy. First, we must begin with a new attitude of willingness to manage our differences constructively.

Finding the Mind of Christ

A church can turn its conflict into a process for finding the mind of God in a matter. If this is done rather than have one side "win" and another "lose" in a dispute, both can benefit through the process. However, this may be done only when the struggle is understood as a procedure, not an end in itself. We do not strive to "win"; rather we labor to find the mind of Christ.

Discord Is Inevitable

The second beneficial attitude accepts discord as inevitable. Conflicts in human relations are inescapable. The Christian physician-author Paul Tournier reminds us:

> It is not possible for people to work together at a common task without there being differences of opinion, conflicts, jealousy and bitterness. And in a religious organization they are less willing to bring these differences out into the open. They feel quite sin-

> cerely that as Christians they ought to be showing a spirit of forgiveness, charity and mutual support. The aggressiveness is repressed, taking the form of anxiety.[1]

The Bible is a study of conflict. In Genesis, Satanic argument brings death to the human race. Dissension permeates the Old Testament. In the New Testament discordant notes of strife sound from beginning to end. There is a theology of conflict in these pages. Our salvation is an obvious personal battle. Jesus gave instructions for individual behavior when faced with differences. Luke 22:24 records how even the disciples were not free from quarrels. Acts is a history of contentions in the early church. The writings of Paul, especially 1 and 2 Corinthians, give guidance to Christians in disagreement. Look again at Paul's formula for confronting variance: "Be on the alert [be aware], stand firm in the faith, be brave, be strong. Do all your work in love" (1 Cor. 16:13-14, GNB). Be aware that inevitably there is going to be discord. Be alert to deal with it in love.

Some Benefits of Conflict

Another helpful attitude basic to confronting differences is to see the good sides of conflict. A clash may indicate that there are sterling qualities active in a church. This view may seem to be a "whistling in the dark," but it's not.

Several years ago our church faced the need to move from its old location. We bought property and began an extension ministry. Our congregation continued to worship at the established church while we developed a new mission and made plans to move. Complex problems resulted in slow progress. Although I yearned to move faster, coercive action would have destroyed good attitudes being formed.

At a deacons' meeting I was surprised by the critical feelings of a few men. Some deacons thought my leadership too conservative. Those men felt that either the church should adopt new plans or get a new pastor—or both. When the chairman tried to slow the rising dispute, one fellow interrupted by pointing a finger at me and shouting, "Preacher, you're a coward! I'm against you all the way. Right or wrong, one way or another I'm going to get rid of you so we can move ahead." This sudden outburst threw the meeting into a confusion like an old western gunfight at a card table. Men pushed their chairs back from the conference table and fled without adjourning formalities. I appealed to the attacker, but he stomped out angrily. I had a hard time believing anything good could come out of that fray. But experience revealed the benefits of that quarrel.

Aggressive discontent may be a revelation of deep concerns among the people. Vitality can be smothered by a pretense of agreement. I know a church which hasn't had a disagreement of any consequence in thirty years. Someone observed, "When the Lord returns, that congregation will ascend ahead of everybody else. For the Scriptures say, 'The dead in Christ shall rise first!'"

Yet, in such a dormant congregation there may be members who disturb the peace because their needs are not being met. Their frustration drives them to protest complacency. Dissatisfaction may be a stirring of life in the church. Struggle can mean there is concern, vigor, and hope.

Also, a confrontation may indicate that you are on the right track. Jesus hinted at this: "Woe unto you, when all men shall speak well of you! for so did their fathers to the false prophets" (Luke 6:26). Paul stated, "If it be possible, as much as lieth in you, live peaceably with all men" (Rom. 12:18). But Paul knew that it is not always possible to be peaceable and righteous at the same time. It is right to oppose evil. Just be careful to behave righteously while contradicting wrong.

A final benefit I'll suggest from conflict is illustrated by a terrible church fight we had. In this agonizing melee both the church and I had a growing experience. We were thrust mentally and spiritually in directions we would never have moved otherwise. The threat of destruction stirred us to find new guidance and support. For every church there are untried fields of knowledge and varied behavior patterns that wait to help. Conflict can stimulate creativity.

The fight I refer to broke out when we fired a staff member. Problems demanding this were discussed over a long period of time before he was dismissed. The personnel committee, deacons, and other key leaders were consulted. Nevertheless, the termination culminated in a furor that refused to subside. Despite a public explanation for the dismissal, an intense emotional schism developed in the congregation. I sought to bring about reconciliations and get the church back to its tasks. Weeks passed, and I realized the only thing happening was a hardening of attitudes. The majority of people were supportive. But the spirit of a church is not built by evaluating majorities.

Things had to improve! But how? An angry spirit paralyzed the church. Everything anybody could think of was tried (almost everything; I stayed). Then, in the providence of God, I was led to a new idea. The plan was radical in its approach.

My recommendation was to employ a qualified counselor. He would come to our church on contract for a limited time. I wanted him to interview a cross section of our membership. These individual interviews were to be confidential. He was to learn why the people were angry. I felt the continuing strife was not simply because we had fired a staff member. We had grievances, but no way to communicate them. At least there was no effective way to which the people would respond. Emotions were turbulent; distrust poisoned relationships; groups polarized.

The church was reluctant to engage anyone for anything at the time. However, there were no alternatives to finding a solution. So we hired him.

The counselor made appointments to talk with many members. He reported general information and impressions without betraying confidences. His reports were to me each week and the deacons each month. His recommendations accompanied these periodic reviews. In one conference he told me of hostile feelings held by members.

"But those feelings are not right. The facts are what count!" I protested.

"John, *feelings are fact.* These attitudes exist, no matter why. That's an important fact you must deal with in resolving this conflict."

I learned an important lesson; it was vital that I knew how people felt and why. Not until I received *the facts of feeling* was I able to work effectively toward a solution. Sometimes a person's *feeling* is a more critical element than *facts* relating to disagreement.

Another benefit came from the counselor's approach to resolving conflict. The counselor was able to convey facts and feelings between people. He spoke as a neutral party without emotional involvement. Soon people began to hear and understand how others felt. This softened attitudes and illuminated opinions which brought peace. Since then we have developed better communication to increase both trust and tolerance.

Now, a final emphasis on this positive attitude. Conflict can generate new power within both church and individuals. This new strength for handling disagreements will aid peace rather than stimulate aggression. My personal development through conflict has increased my ability to resolve differences with happier success than before. This new skill can be attained by individuals and churches.

The Negative Side

Obviously there is a negative side to controversy. The tolerant attitude which allows for disagreement must be alert to its hazards. Later on in this book I'll discuss major harmful consequences of conflict. For now, consider three negative aspects of strife.

The first hazard of controversy is deception. Variance comes upon the scene in acceptable garb. Disagreement justifies its stance and parades spirituality. Although dispute is sometimes justifiable, too often it attacks from hidden motives. The danger is that we will be self-deceived as we oppose someone.

This self-deception is illustrated in a dispute long ago between Newman Smith and the great preacher Robert Hall. They disagreed over some religious point. Smith wrote an invective paper denouncing Hall. Smith could not decide on a title for the pamphlet, so he asked a friend to suggest one. Some time before Smith had written a popular tract entitled "Come to Jesus." When his friend read the violent censure against Hall, he returned the manuscript to Smith with a note. "The title I suggest for your pamphlet is this: 'Go to Hell by the author of Come to Jesus.'"

Contention blinds us to our own faults by focusing on the mistakes of others. Hypocrisy develops as we are unaware that an evil spirit moves within our good intentions.

Conflict is also disruptive. Constructive progress is stopped by variance. "You can't fight a war and build a city at the same time" is a true adage. Bickering drains energy and distracts the mind from worthy goals. Although controversy sometimes stimulates new approaches to problems, strife can smother creativity. Freedom to love and grow and hope is blocked by discord. The extent of a disruption depends on its intensity and scope. Fortunately, a quarrel may be resolved before it spreads to do greater harm.

In my own reaction, discouragement is the greatest negative effect of serious controversy. Strife brings guilt and a sense of failure to me. I've also noticed this feeling among the people, whether they are directly involved in a dispute or not.

Such discouragement cripples churches because it often brings the attitude that someone should quit. A good pastor is pressured to leave. A sincere member is made to feel unwanted. Other discouraged people withdraw into grieved inactivity. Conflict should be managed to ease the sense of personal failure and give encouragement.

IBM teaches assembly operators to control their attitudes and work effectively with imperfect parts. They wanted to learn, and they did. In the church, members must *want to learn* ways to work out their disagreements happily. They must believe that learning and change is better than bungling along from one offense to another.

Although disagreement is a continual reality, ability to manage conflict is the most lacking of all social skills. We slip into strife unaware of its cause. Dispute is then fueled by ignorance until it flames out of control. Because there are few opportunities for learning how to handle conflict, the church should provide training situations. Disagreements must not destroy the spirit of harmony in the church. We can learn to handle our differences.

Some people are threatened by the phrase *managing conflict*. To them it implies manipulation. In my use, *manage* means discovering and using ways to control a dispute so that the disagreement ultimately concludes in peace and righteousness. Such guidance can be learned. Management is not subtle manipulation; neither does it imply suppression. Rather, it is channeling rival forces so that the least harm is done, and the most good is accomplished. Effective supervision may not conclude a dispute quickly. The wise procedure may be to work through disagreements until eventually there is unity rather than concession. Church leaders must learn ways of managing conflict effectively.

If I have belabored the inevitability of conflict, I do not mean to imply that continuing tension is normal. To the contrary, a persistent spirit of strife will cripple a church. My emphasis at this point is: Be tolerant enough to face disagreements without being afraid, and correct them without being ashamed.

3

Confusion: Cause of Conflict

A church fight may be compared to a burning building. To the casual observer, a house on fire is total confusion. The untrained person doesn't know how to put it out. All he knows is that the heat's uncomfortable, and something valuable is being destroyed. But trained firemen recognize the type of fire and what is needed to extinguish it. Similarly, handling controversy begins with some knowledge of its types and causes. Three basic types of conflict are: impersonal, intrapersonal, and interpersonal.

Impersonal conflicts are about facts, values, goals and methods. These conflicts relate to doctrine and how to make beliefs work. Whether to build; how to raise money; where to place the piano; these are impersonal matters.

Intrapersonal conflict takes place within a person. Each individual struggles with his own attitudes. Inward debates occur over beliefs and feelings. For example: When a person becomes frustrated, he often battles with guilt feelings within himself. Paul Tournier wisely observes, "There is no life without conflict; no conflict without guilt."[1]

In this intrapersonal arena energies muster for an open attack to divert attention from our own inner struggles. Edward Lindaman states that a person can handle almost anything "except not being clear in one's own mind concerning what he believes."[2] When I'm uncertain about my genuine attitude and under pressure to "do something," I either have mental paralysis or hyperactivity. Neither solves the problem, but it does divert attention from my own inward conflict.

The deacons of Rockridge Baptist Church chastened their pastor because he did not visit "enough." Fact was, the deacons were indecisive about a family ministry program assigned them. So they eased their own sense of guilt by finding fault with the pastor. On the other side of this coin, when a pastor neglects his "duties," he may relieve guilt feelings by condemning the congregation for their failures. Intrapersonal tensions often evolve into open, interpersonal strife.

Interpersonal conflicts are between people. Feelings often dominate attitudes and break into personal attacks. Clashes occur among staff members in competition for privileges or recognition. Power struggles for positions of influence are common in most organizations. Personal grievances over petty differences are in this category.

Besides knowing something about the types of controversy, the ability to recognize *causes* is essential. Reasons for disputes are as varied as the people who quarrel. Disagreements are seldom simple, but four causes of conflict I have known are: confusion, concealment, control, communication. I shall discuss these causes in chapters that follow.

One common cause of controversy is confusion. There is a unique difficulty in dealing with this source of trouble because confusion produces frustration; frustration generates anger; and anger blinds. People hate to admit they are confused, lest they show their ignorance. In defensive pride they take a strong stance for their opinion; then committed, they fight for it.

For several generations there had been strife between two factions in a rural church. When Reverend Purdum came as pastor, no one told him there was discord. Soon after coming he was caught in a tug-of-war between the two groups. This time it was a struggle over plans to enlarge the sanctuary. The young minister appointed people from each faction to a building committee, and he presided over it. Deadlock!

In frustration Rev. Purdum stopped calling committee meetings while he sought reasons for the hostility. Two families, the Carouthers and Haldanes, formed cores of opposing cliques. Several generations before Purdum's time the church had purchased a new piano. The Carouthers and Haldanes disagreed about where to place it. The dispute outlasted the piano! Now there was a Hammond organ and no piano. Still, both families and their friends continued to clash over everything. When asked why, no one really knew. An old-timer replied, "Well, best I can tell, it's just a case of the gingham dog and the calico cat." They were all confused and didn't know the reason; nor would they face it. Confusion blinded them to their real problem.

Although there are numerous attitudes which foster confusion, I have noticed three which predominate. The mental conditions of ignorance, distortion, and mood generate confusion.

Ignorance

Supreme Court Justice Louis Brandeis wrote, "Behind every argument is someone's ignorance."[3] Ignorance is a primary element in confusion. Many people, upset about a matter, do not have all the facts. Or they ignore reality. Either way, confusion is created and tensions develop.

Years ago I presided over our church's business meeting when the budget committee made its annual recommendation. The committee had studied every factor carefully. It was not the usual repetition of last year's plans, with minor adjustments.

The paper was distributed to the people and discussion was permitted. Ignorance immediately took the floor, and Emotion encouraged him with loud amens! Confusion spread when Mrs. Blarney arose with a strong protest. She objected angrily to the secretary's small salary increase and to the janitor being paid too much. Mrs. Blarney didn't know any facts about their work patterns. Fact was, the secretary should have been dismissed, but she had too many relatives in the congregation to permit such a sensible move. The discussion became a squabble. Facts were silenced, ignorance prevailed, charity fled, confusion reigned.

Distortion

Distortion also brings confusion. Each of us views facts through his own personal filter. We look at identical images through the flawed lenses of our individual experiences. So an unpleasant incident with a pastor may distort ability to judge the next one fairly. Even good memories color attitudes. Sometimes what we liked at our former church is not present in the new one. This can distort our attitude toward everything else in the church.

Mood

Confusion from ignorance and distortion may be intensified by the present mood of society. Elizabeth Skoglund points this out in her book *To Anger with Love*. "The rapid change of values in our society has contributed to a general sense of frustration. People seem unsure of who they are and what they should be doing. Even when they seem right, they feel wrong."[4]

This malaise invades the church and sometimes overwhelms the spirit of Christ within us. Stirred by the temper of the world about us, our spirit becomes frustrated. Frustration leads to anger, and anger generates a hostile mood. So controversy is the norm today. If you don't like a situation, change it. If you disagree, protest! If you are unhappy, split! Defy! Strike! Rebel! Do your own thing; you've got your rights! This turbulent spirit of the world infects our behavior in the church.

Unfortunately, we seldom realize that there is confusion when we are in a dispute. We want to believe everything is clear-cut. We are blinded to ignorance, distortion, and moods. Instead, "something wrong" or "somebody" gets the blame. But confusion is to blame, and that blinding fog is hard to dispel.

Roles

Conflict caused by confusion in my experience has been in two areas: roles and goals. Church members function in many different ways within the fellowship. A "role" is a pattern of activity fulfilling a particular responsibility. Example: One duty of a pastor is to be the preacher. A secretary may have several assignments; she may keep records, handle correspondence, and be a receptionist. However, someone may have the post of receptionist exclusively, without being a secretary. Roles are joined to specific tasks; this needs to be understood by everyone who serves the church.

Paul illustrated roles in the church by referring to a human body (1 Cor. 12). Parts of the body have different tasks. The eye is responsible for seeing and the ear for hearing. Each member of the body must perform a helpful service. So members of the church, having different spiritual abilities, should serve in various ways.

Confusion arises when people do not recognize the place of roles within the church body. One factor obscuring the function of limited offices is a wrong emphasis on "the believer's priesthood." This precious doctrine teaches our access to God without a human mediator. It also implies an equality before God among all believers. However, it is mistaken by some as an open door to any activity a member may wish to assume in the church.

Because believers share a certain equality, some suppose they may exercise any privilege they wish. Such freedom is not inferred in this doctrine. A priest is concerned largely with vertical relationships. The believer's priesthood does not convey horizontal prerogatives which ignore different roles of responsibility. Romans 12 and 1 Corinthians 12 affirm that we can be equal without being identical. Although equal in standing before God, we are not the same in our functions within the body of Christ. Each member is a part of the body and shares in its life. However, each member is limited in what it can do. The foot is not to do the work of a hand. An ear is no substitute for the eye. This analogy is applied to the church by Paul. The "priesthood of the believer" is valid. But that truth does not abrogate clear teachings that unique gifts of the Spirit are used in specific roles within the church.

Roles function to fulfill responsibilities. Responsibilities are inseparable from accountability. In the church we are accountable to those from whom we draw our ability to function. As a part of the body of Christ we cannot ignore other members just because we appeal to our relationships with God. His concern is the welfare of the church; so ours must be. Thus our dedication should express itself in responsible relationship through specific roles. Each role is accountable to an authority outside itself. When we ignore this and function "on our own," conflict ultimately arises.

Presumptions

Role conflicts are caused by presumptions and pressures. When a worker presumes that he is to function in a certain way, he may contradict what others expect. This often occurs when there is a lack of information about the task.

A role conflict arose in one church because members of the music committee presumed they were to engage a new music minister. Without consulting anyone they took the initiative to seek a director. When the personnel committee learned about it they reacted angrily. Fortunately the pastor managed the conflict and avoided a destructive clash.

In part this presumption may have occurred because the music committee had not been instructed about its duties. Perhaps they did not know who was responsible for hiring a staff member.

An imperative for every church is a continuing education of its members to the tasks of ministry. When new programs are developed, people are alert to fresh procedures. However, the established work by old committees is often presumed to be understood. The church must instruct new members and remind experienced workers of what is and what is not to be done.

Presumption may emerge from ambition for power. If we want a position or privilege intensely, we already see ourselves functioning in that capacity. It is easy to step into the role which is not really ours.

Eric had served on the finance committee in another church. He wanted the same position in the church where he is now a member. Instead he was elected to serve on the property committee. Someone made a suggestion that the entrance to the church grounds needed to be illuminated. The property committee met to discuss the request. Eric wanted to talk first about the expense and the general financial condition of the church.

"How do we know we can afford a lighted sign?" growled Eric.

"Eric, why don't we discuss whether we feel there is a real need and what type of light would be best?" replied the chairman.

"There's no point in wasting our time talking if the church shouldn't spend the money on such foolishness."

"That's the responsibility of the budget control committee, Eric. Let them wrestle with that."

A quarrel ensued over money. Eric was not willing to work within his role but presumed to make financial decisions.

Pressure

Pressures often confuse our understanding of roles and cause explosive encounters. Expectations are one form of such pressure.

People "expect" the pastor to perform certain services, so he is under pressure to do them. He is expected to preach helpful sermons. It is understood that he'll comfort the grieved and visit the sick. The pastor fills various roles for his people. Sometimes he is overwhelmed with the pressures from many directions. Some members hope he'll handle matters which are not his responsibility. They want him to serve in roles that are not his, or for which he is not fitted. The pastor may be a man for all seasons, but he cannot be a man for all services.

The women's missionary society was having a luncheon meeting in the basement of our church. One of the ladies opened a kitchen cabinet; there was a dead mouse! In horror she gasped, "Somebody go upstairs and get the pastor to come down here and carry this dead mouse out of our kitchen!"

Mrs. Hampton spoke up: "No indeed, we will not! God did not call our pastor to carry dead mice from the church kitchen." So Mrs. Hampton carried it out herself.

The courage of that elderly lady saved me from one role conflict by improper pressures. Since then I have often wished for other Mrs. Hamptons to divert wrong expectations.

Confusion about roles is a common cause of friction within a church fellowship. Instruction and spiritual discipline are needed to keep us working effectively within our roles.

Goals

A second area where I have seen confusion develop into controversy has been in the function of goals in the church program. A church without goals for its programs is adrift without chart or compass. Also, too many projects among organizations creates another kind of confusion. The failure to have defined aims which unite the people leaves a church vulnerable to conflict.

Most members do not know what their church is supposed to accomplish. Without clearly stated goals people cannot know what they should do. Christians want to feel significant; but if their church has no objectives, what is there to do? All that is left is "playing church" with insignificant activities.

Without purpose there is no spirit of working together among the people. When there are no stated intentions of ministry, the confusion about roles is added to the bewilderment of purpose.

A church with too many goals can be as deranged as one without any. Divergent aims emerge when members insist on an individuality to do as each feels led. In such a church voices call from many directions.

"The gospel needs to be demonstrated in a caring ministry to the multitudes" is an undeniable appeal.

"I think our church needs to major on evangelism" can always be heard.

Another threatens, "If we don't start emphasizing missions, I'm going to organize my own."

"Worship is the central, upward thrust of all believers" gets a good hearing.

"Small groups really communicate practical Christianity" is a claim that is valid.

Granted, the Bible teaches a diversity of gifts of the Spirit for the church. However, a local body of believers needs to establish agreed upon goals. Otherwise, it will fragment and fight or dissipate resources on limited efforts. Goals help clarify its purpose for a church.

Failure

Simply stated, goal setting is deciding *what* should be done and *when*. After that the *who* and *how* are planned. That sounds simple enough. Then why do so many churches fail to set goals? For the same reason so few individuals have personal goals. I have been such a person. One of my life's great failures has been too few goals. I've looked back and wondered why. There are several reasons. My personal reasons for not setting more goals are the same that hinder some churches.

The first cause of my failure to be goal oriented: I was not taught it. I was not told how; nor was it modeled by anyone close to me. When I was nine years old, the great depression fell upon us. From then until I was twenty, I was conditioned to a philosophy of survival. For our family to get by was a big accomplishment. The possibility for anything more than survival was not introduced into my thinking during those formative days. Similarly, many churches have not been taught the advantages of planning to do great things for God. They feel that if they are at peace and have their bills paid, that's enough.

One strong religious influence during my young adult years kept me from planning goals. In my spiritual life, I was taught to avoid thinking of "things" (they are worldly). "If God wants you to have anything, he'll provide it." I learned not to think in terms of the specific and concrete (that's limiting God). "The spiritual life is not related to measurable concepts." These are not the exact words, but they distill the essence of what came through to me. Many Christians separate the "spiritual" from the "practical" and so never set measurable attainments for their faith.

That particular religious influence spawned another error which deterred me from projecting goals. That error equated activity with accomplishment. It didn't matter whether my being busy achieved anything or not. Results were not my concern, I thought. Churches think this way too, and it sets the stage to squabble over merely "doing something." Then they get into arguments over *means* rather than *goals.*

One time in our church we had a controversy over buying a bus. Someone proposed, "We ought to have a bus!"

"Why?"

"Well, nearly every church in town has a bus ministry. We need a bus."

The details of a bus ministry were ignored. Specifically what we wanted to accomplish with a bus was never decided. No one would take the responsibility for a bus ministry. We had confused means with goals. The bus was a means for doing certain things, but we did not define what we wanted to accomplish.

Finally we bought a big, new bus. But we've never developed an effective bus ministry. We've picked up a few people in the neighborhood, taken some trips, but that's all. Now we realize there's a lot of money in equipment that's not being used effectively. We confused means with goals and equated activity with accomplishment.

A primary reason for my being slow to project goals was the fear of failure. *What if I set a target and miss? Suppose I plan to reach an objective and fail? I may choose a goal and circumstances keep me from reaching it.*

I was afraid of what some people would think. But a deeper fear was how I would feel about myself. I had a low self-image and didn't want to get knocked down again by failure. I feared another mark in the fail column. Then I learned that, even with failures, I'd have more in the win column by setting goals than by playing it safe. When Babe Ruth held the record for the most home runs, he also held the record for the most strikeouts. But it's the home runs people remember.

I used another excuse for failing to name objectives: *I can get along without them; I really don't need them.* For one reason or another, I did not want something enough. Then I noticed in the Scriptures that Jesus asked people, "What do you want?" (Matt. 20:32; Mark 10:51; John 5:6). Our Lord helped those who declared their desires. He did *not* help those who did not want his gifts.

Reflecting on my own "contentment" (and I often hid behind Phil. 4:11), I really didn't want to do what it would take to reach a particular goal. How often I've heard this in meetings with church folk: "We don't need this." "We can get along without that." What they really meant was, "We don't want to do what it will take to reach a higher level of attainment." "We'd rather do without it than make the sacrifice to get it." When we do not have goals, we are relieved of effort and commitment.

The absence of goals leaves a church without direction. It brings confusion to people wanting to serve and sets the stage for serious conflict.

4

Concealment: Cause of Conflict

"Concealment," wrote Shakespeare, "is like a worm in the bud." Its destructive work is hidden by something acceptable. Church problems are complicated by our tendency to ignore the real motive for our actions. Causes of conflict are often purposefully hidden behind agreeable "reasons." Sometimes a controversy grows without anyone's awareness of its impetus.

I believe more disagreements come out of feelings than fact. There is one reason for this: The church is an emotional arena. For many people, religion is more sentiment than truth, and matters are frequently determined by impulse rather than reason. The actual seed for congregational dissension is often unknown because roots of strife lie deep within the personalities of people.

Much of the conflict I have faced has worn an innocent mask at first. The rationale of its origin was camouflaged. If some general areas of concealment can be identified here, they may guide us to quicker solutions—or at least to prudent behavior. Although there are many covert motives, I group my experience with the hidden cause of controversy in three categories. They are: the Watts syndrome, the smoke screen, the programmed script.

The Watts Syndrome

The burning of the Watts area in Los Angeles was a tragic protest. After the riot Martin Luther King walked through Watts. He met a group of small boys on the street. "We won, we won!" they shouted. King asked them, "How can you say you won when thirty-four Negroes are dead, your community is destroyed, and whites are using the riot as an excuse for inaction?" Their reply was: "We won because we made them pay attention to us."

The desire for recognition stirs in every person. It is an urge to sustain personal dignity. However, this craving often drives a person to extremes, as in the Watts riot—and church fights.

Church is the only place where some poeple have an opportunity for recognition. They are ignored at home; their job gives them little exposure; and their social life is that of a back-row spectator. In church, as a child of God, they should get some recognition. When that doesn't happen, resentment sometimes breaks out in a church quarrel.

As the congregation gathered for a business meeting Mabel screeched to her friend, "I've got a vote just like anyone else! I've got a right to speak, even if I am not an officer of the church." Normally Mabel was a compliant person. She held no responsibility except being the wife of a domineering husband. But at church she ascended controversy's podium and gained attention.

Beside the need for recognition, the Watts syndrome indicates needs not being met. *Status quo* reigns! "We've always done it this way" prevails. When people become frustrated at not getting their needs considered, they may join *any* fray to shake the existing structure. Then controversy may direct attention to both a need for ministry and the starved ego.

The Smoke Screen

The smoke screen hides a score of reasons for dissension. A person may protest one matter while he is, in fact, angry about another. The fire is hidden by the smoke.

Pride often ignites strife and hides behind acceptable complaints. Mr. Dickens was a successful businessman, but the church he attended was not growing. It was in a location of limited opportunities. Dickens had a brother-in-law at a congregation booming with activity and additions. This was too much for pride to bear. So Dickens began a controversial movement to change the leadership of his church, "so we can get things going for the Lord."

Guilt is another emotion cloaking its shame behind aggressive distractions. The Valeside community congregation assigned their Sunday School officers a specific task of enlarging membership. This meant planning, enlistment, and visitation; but the officers simply did not want to do the required work. They were embarrassed at having to report nothing accomplished. So these workers began a distracting tactic by criticizing the director of Youth activities. The ensuing fight over firing this young man got attention off the Sunday School leaders.

Pain over some personal, inner conflict drives others into a dispute. Mr. Elder, chairman of the church board, started a movement to dismiss their pastor. Reason? "The people need a stronger pulpit ministry. Our pastor is not an effective preacher. If he'd preach more on the will of God, my son might go into the ministry. I may have felt the call to preach, but I wasn't sure. I want my son to hear God's call; this preacher isn't helping."

Elder's friend replied, "Could it be you are really saying, 'I'm still hurting. If my son would go into the ministry, I'd feel I was making it up to God. But the pastor's preaching is not getting him into the Lord's service. The pastor is hindering me; if I remove him, I'll get rid of my remorse.' Is this what you are really saying?"

As Elder talked this out with his friend he began to see the hidden forces driving him. He faced the responsibility for his own mistakes and quit trying to make his son's decisions. Elder was also courageous enough to initiate reconciliation with his pastor.

Of all hidden motives for variance, the most secret is envy. Envy is a sin no one readily admits. It is the meanest cause of disagreement within the body of Christ. Envy plagued the disciples with the question, "Who among us will be greatest?" It even caused the crucifixion of Jesus (Matt. 27:18; Mark 15:10). Envy distorts that teaching of the Bible which says that we are all equal before God. It equates being equal with being identical. Envy does not want anyone to have anything it does not possess.

Henry Fairlie dissects envy in his classic essays, *The Seven Deadly Sins Today.* "Envy is a source of discord . . . a sower of strife between neighbors, even between friends. It introduces into even the most straightforward of relationships an atmosphere of distrust . . . until even the most amiable will find they also have fangs."[1]

Everything good may become an object of envy's secret attacks. Membership on a committee, a talent to serve, status in the community, promotion at work, some scrap of good luck are all viewed by envy's jaundiced eye. "We even envy someone who is good!" writes Fairlie. "We will not believe that they are good, or that they are as good as they seem, or that they are good for the right reasons."[2]

Although I've recognized envy's ugly presence in many disputes, I do not know how to deal with it in another person. Its disguises protect envy. The only place I can effectively confront envy is in myself. Leslie H. Farber gives good advice: "The most pressing concern in regard to so damaging and disturbing an affliction as envy, is not so much to ponder when, or even why, it may originally come into being, as to discover it now where it is, to outwit its distractions and disguises, to measure its fear of being called by name."[3] When envy raises up within me, and I call it by name, then I can struggle against it.

The Programmed Script

Psychologists refer to a learned behavior pattern as a "script." We are conditioned to give unconscious responses to certain stimuli. Children learn to react emotionally in a given way, and our actions are frequently controlled by these subconscious directives.

The church has two kinds of people behaving from their scripts rather than living by the Spirit. First, there is the undeveloped Christian. A great problem in the church today is its multitude of immature Christians. They have not grown in grace and knowledge of Christ; they are still infants in the faith. Some of them are very old infants!

Childish behavior in an adult is often the extension of inadequate family life. Many Christians handle problems at church the way they face conflict in their homes. "The family is, after all, the prototype of all organizations and becomes the primative referent for the individual in his later work experience in organizations," writes Zaleznik.[4]

Institutions that influence children the most are the home and the school. Encounter patterns are learned there. The fragmentation of home life and the prevailing rebelliousness in public schools give poor models for peaceable conflict resolutions.

Too often a member tries to settle his disagreements in church the way he learned at home and school. Then church becomes an extension of the world's hostility rather than a sanctuary from strife. We function from a script programmed without God.

The second example in script behavior is the unregenerate church member. He has no directive for his actions other than his sinful nature. He is programmed to self, not to Christ. Like it or not, this is a constant factor in the church.

Whether the script of an unregenerate person or an immature Christian is played out, the point is the same: They have not learned to seek the mind of Christ and act accordingly. They play out their own script.

Lester is a classic example of man living by programmed script. He united with our church after leaving a congregation in angry disagreement with the pastor. (I learned this *after* he joined us.) Over a year after Lester came we had a crisis with a staff member quitting. Lester was a vocal and intense critic of the leadership involved in that dispute.

One day I confronted him in private. "Lester, your behavior puzzles me. You had not shown any interest in this man before. In fact, you have been very critical of him. I cannot imagine that you care whether he stayed or left the church. I don't understand your hostility in this matter. Would you explain it to me?"

Lester stared at me in silence for several moments, then replied, "You're right, preacher, I don't care. But I've been mad at you for a long time, and this is my first chance to get at you."

Soon after that incident, Lester joined another church. There he helped a group pressure the pastor to resign. Lester functions from a programmed script of hostility toward pastors.

The Watts syndrome, the smoke screen, and the programmed script suggest only a few patterns of concealing motives. Our personalities are so complex we're unaware of all the influences that move us. Most of us are more devious than we'll admit.

5

Control of Power: Cause of Conflict

Conflict is intimately related to power. Every conflict involves the use of power. But no organization can exist or function without power, and the church is an organization.

Power is an offensive word when used in a personal relationship. If we say a person has "power," this implies influence over people. In the church, *power* is an ugly word unless we can spiritualize it. We like to say a person has "power in prayer." We delight when someone has "great power with the Lord," but resent it if he has power on a finance committee. We figure God can take care of himself, but we've got to protect the money! By our very complaint of another's power, we covet it for ourselves. Hence comes conflict.

What is meant by "power"? Power is simply the ability to get things done. Power is whatever produces an effect. In the arena of human relations, power is whatever causes a response.

Power comes in many forms and from an infinite number of sources. Power does ultimately come from God; but power also comes from people. Power comes from logic and emotion, from fact and superstitions, from knowledge and fantasy. There is number power and money power; there is *status quo* power and venture power; there is reputation power and authority power. Whatever causes response has in it the resources from which power is formed. But these resources are inert until used by a person. That person's attitude determines how he will use the resource. Power is then generated when resource and attitude are fused to effect a response.

There's an old saying, "Power corrupts." Yes, but power also purifies; Jesus used it so. Power deprives, but power also provides.

Power destroys, but power also constructs. Power is necessary to accomplish anything. It is the use of power that determines its character.

In the church many kinds of power are constantly working. Where there are relationships of people, power ebbs and flows. Conflict sometimes results from this power in action. From my own experience I see power as the cause of conflict from four perspectives. (1) Conflict arises from the abuse of power, (2) in the assignment of power, (3) upon the assumption of power, and (4) in the absence of power.

The Abuse of Power

Many church conflicts are protests against the abuse of power. Sometimes those outside leadership groups try to break into the power structure. One entrance is through flaws in the way power is administered. But this is not always so. Sometimes those in sympathy with the leadership see abuses of power and seek to correct it. Such disagreements often evolve into discord.

By the abuse of power I mean the abuse of relationships and responsibilities. I've watched power abused, suffered under it, and at times indulged in the misuse of power in two primary ways: by domination and by intimidation.

Power is sometimes preserved *by dominating* whatever relates to it. This is done in an infinite number of ways. One common abuse of power is the guarding of *status quo*. In a church I served during student days, one man controlled the church. He had great influence in the community as well as in the church. Many people in the congregation needed credit from him sometime, so they didn't protest his control at church. Mr. Bullock's favorite expression seemed to be, "Preachers come, and preachers go." He kept the *status quo*.

Another example of guarding the *status quo* is sometimes seen upon the change of pastors. The members who were close to the former minister and wielded dominant leadership may not want to share that power. If the new pastor disagrees with their ways or seeks to bring other members into leadership positions, strife sometimes ensues.

Withholding information is a subtle way of dominating. It is obvious that all information should certainly not be mailed out in the weekly newsletter. However, sometimes vital information is too controlled. The treasurer of a church I served gave no accounting to anyone. He picked up the Sunday contributions, deposited them, and paid the bills. When a project was proposed of which he did not approve, Clint merely said, "We don't have the money to do it." When I pressed him for information, tension developed. Eventually the congregation began regular business meetings, and information was made available. Then the power began to be shared.

A devious way of dominating is to avoid planning. A pastor can dominate in decision making if he avoids making plans. Or he can make plans without involving people in the process.

Then there is domination by decree. This is done by using stringent rules. Up-to-date bylaws are necessary to administer a church effectively. However, as with all laws, they impose limitations. Sometimes the limitations attempt to be explicit about every detail. Then those people expected to work under the rules are controlled beyond reason. Most dominating decrees are reactions to former excesses.

A church suffered from a pastor who spent funds irresponsibly. The congregation reacted radically. They passed a rule that every expenditure over fifty dollars must have congregational approval. They exerted their power to dominate by decree. The result was a paralysis in administration. Controversy developed, and the church was hurt before a reasonable adjustment was made.

Finally, power can dominate by refusing to reconcile differences. Most congregationally governed churches settle their differences by a win/lose vote. This has likely emerged from the false concept that a New Testament church is to be "democratic." So we have adopted political patterns of behavior and sought to solve everything by a win/lose vote. Granted, there must be some mechanics of learning people's wish in a matter. But often we ignore the Scriptures which admonish the church "That ye all speak the same thing, and that there be no divisions among you; but that ye be perfectly joined together in the same mind and in the same judgment" (1 Cor. 1:10; see also Mark 9:50; Rom. 14:19; 1 Thess. 5:13; Eph. 3:13). However, it is easier to vote than to seek the mind of Christ. It takes time to develop harmony and act under the guidance of the Spirit. It is also easier to control power by refusing to work at problems than to find an agreeable solution in the spirit of goodwill.

Power also abuses by *intimidation*. Power can influence by fear, but power's abuse by generating fear destroys love. For just as love casts out fear (1 John 4:18), so fear crushes love. Fear paralyzes communication and with its silence closes the door to relationships.

Intimidation can be brazen, but it is often sly. It seeks to entrap with crafty questions and threatens by artful insinuations. Within the church there are two ways of intimidating which are used frequently. People intimidate others by withdrawing relationships and by withholding power.

The quiet withdrawal from a relationship can intimidate the person left. Here we use silence as a weapon. Keep verbal communication to a minimum. Leave the church by a different exit. Neglect the usual greetings. When such action from influential leaders in our church becomes obvious to me, my stomach tightens.

"What's wrong? What did I do? Why are they avoiding me?"

I sometimes take a defensive attitude toward those withdrawing. If I make an effort to talk with them but get a reserved response, fear touches me. Silence intimidates.

In the early years of my ministry, our church engaged a seminary student to serve part-time as a minister of education. He worked hard and brought progressive changes to our Sunday School. The *status quo* people complained, and opposition to change arose. The Sunday School continued to grow, but so did criticism.

This criticism angered me, so I decided to defend the student. This I did at a business meeting of the congregation. I was young and inexperienced in reconciling such problems, so I used a hammer to swat a fly. I put the spotlight on the sideshow instead of the main event, a growing Sunday School. At the close of my talk I asked for comments from the people. Silence. After the benediction, people moved quickly and silently out. I suddenly realized their silence was a harbinger of trouble to come. For several weeks the leaders spoke with me very little. We had a hard time for a while. Since then I've been very sensitive to sudden or unusual silence among people.

Another mode of intimidation is to withhold doing good. It's a common practice to withhold money as a method of wielding power.

If the offerings drop, some members take that as a sign that God's blessing are not upon the church.

Some people withhold their service as well as substance. I served a small church where the treasurer was the power broker. If he did not grant power, progress was thwarted. In a business meeting the congregation voted to spend money on a project this treasurer did not favor. As an exercise of power, he resigned. His status in the church and community threatened anyone who considered taking that vacated position. With no one authorized to sign checks, the church was paralyzed by this resignation. The only solution was a poor one; we elected a man as treasurer who was indifferent to everyone's attitude. But this did circumvent the power broker and kept the church functioning financially.

Most people are less threatening than that treasurer when they withhold their service. They may feign a consideration of others: "Let somebody else serve in that position." Some use fatigue or overwork as their excuse when their intent is to intimidate the leadership.

Of course, there are valid reasons for resignations, no denying that. However, the intentional weakening of an organization by withholding help is an abuse of power. It certainly intimidates those responsible for leading an effective organization.

When people are intimidated or dominated, there will eventually be a reaction. It may come in the form of resistance by conflict. They may respond by quietly leaving the organization. In either event, when power is misused, it wounds rather than strengthens the church.

The Assignment of Power

Much of the power exercised in a church is assigned by some source of authority. It is assigned power. In a congregationally governed church, the members designate certain authority to groups of individuals. If such a church is well organized, power will be channeled to proper people to get a job done.

Power needs to be assigned unequally. This makes possible the managing of potential conflict. When every person has equal power, the scene is set for either paralysis or chaos. Yet it is this inequality

FIRST BAPTIST CHURCH LIBRARY
16TH & "O" STS., N.W.
WASHINGTON, D.C. 20036

which causes conflict at times. If a person does not get the power he wants he may contest his limitations. When there are disagreements over goals and methods, the assignment of authority-power is critical. Assignment must be made so that conflict may be managed. Otherwise, the organization's purpose may be thwarted.

Yet, in the church the assignment of power is one of the most common sources of conflict. There is one reason for this: Authority is often carelessly assigned. This results in excessive power, ambiguous power, and exclusive power.

Excessive power is found in different forms. One of the most common types is a person who has too much responsibility. That person has been assigned too many positions. This often happens when the assigning group does not bother to develop ways of distributing tasks of the church among more people. It is easier to give jobs to the proven workers.

One day when everything was going happily in our church I began to hear disturbing remarks. "The preacher's crowd is running the church." "Look who always gets elected." "Joe is running the church." "Joe is the big ramrod on the board."

I looked at the list of workers in our church. Joe did have more positions than anyone—twelve! But he had always been willing and enthusiastic when asked to take a task. Excessive power had gravitated to him. Fortunately, Joe had not yet been hurt by excessive power. Neither was he burned out with too much church work. One of these two conditions usually happens to people who carry excessive power.

We eased the discontent over Joe's prominence by assuring that corrections would be made. We then looked at all the people elected in light of how many responsibilities they had. We considered one church's method for maintaining balanced leadership. That church had grouped its elected positions into certain categories and assigned points to each office. Those with greater responsibility carried more points: for example, a deacon or Sunday School teacher. Lesser responsibilities carried fewer points. A member was allowed to hold several positions if he did not exceed a certain number of points. This complex system worked splendidly for that church, but we did not use it. We developed a simpler approach, but we did limit the assignment of authority.

Another kind of power assigned that causes conflict is *ambiguous power*. It occurs when a person is elected to an office, but the limits of authority are not defined; nor are responsibilities described. When this happens the door is left open for that person to write his own job description.

A church elected the president for the choir. Although there was a paid music minister, the president saw himself responsible for the music program. In the mind of the new president, that title endued him with complete authority.

The result of this ambiguity was constant discord. The minister of music finally resigned. When the pastor and personnel committee began to interview prospective replacements, the president demanded that he be consulted *first*. "The church elected me as president of the choir, and I'm not going to be a figurehead!" A diplomatic pastor eased the tension and included the president without giving him complete control.

One of the outcomes of this experience was that before the new minister of music was engaged, a complete job description was written for him. Also, an outline of the functions for elected offices within the choir was adopted. Ambiguity is an open range for trouble, with no fences to confine dissension.

Every organization must have a process for assigning persons to places of responsibility. This is done by nominating, electing, or appointing someone for a task. This authority to assign is also the power to exclude. But when assignment power works harder to exclude than it does to include, trouble will come.

Authority to assign should concentrate on making the best selection for a position. Then the person less qualified would be naturally passed by rather than pointedly excluded. The power to assign is abused when exclusion becomes its primary function. Exclusive power usually results from a negative attitude rather than a positive approach to solving problems.

Exclusive power is defensive and develops a fortress mentality. It is strong to defend, but slow to pursue reconciliation. Exclusive power is often motivated by fear, so it shuts the door to communication.

I have exercised exclusive power—sometimes because I was afraid and did not know what more to do. An extreme example—and fortunately a rare one—happened many years ago. In our church there was a person intensely opposed to me. Where it was possible she took action and thwarted any recommendation I favored. Every proposal, any program, almost every deed of mine, was criticized. She was influential in her Sunday School group and used her influence as a podium to enlist opposition. Wherever her influence touched, tension developed, and the spirit of reconciliation died. I sought to discuss our differences but received only arrogance in response.

I discussed this with the deacons and declared myself closed to any further pursuit of relationship. "I learned when I was a boy that if you try to kiss a girl several times and she doesn't kiss back, she's telling you something!" When the nominating committee met, I stated my opposition to that woman holding any position until we could work together harmoniously.

I realized this was an autocratic use of exclusive power. But I believe the pastor is called to shepherd the flock. Sometimes shepherding means protecting the peace. Members do not have the right to fight. Disagreement is allowed, but dissension is not a privilege within the body of Christ (Rom. 14:19; Eph. 4:3; 1 Thess. 5:13).

In the providence of God, the result of excluding this contentious member was that she sought reconciliation. Forgiveness was exchanged and a happy relationship built.

Exclusive power often develops from competition within the church. Occasionally members feel there needs to be an "opposition party." "Somebody needs to be against the preacher" was the way one man expressed his feelings. I believe this feeling of need for an opposing group has evolved from a long emphasis on "democratic processes" within the church. We have taken our pattern of behavior from the world. If there is a democratic expression from the people, we have concluded that there must be at least a two-party system in the church.

There needs to be a feeling of freedom of expression for every member. However, the idea that there must be some in opposition to the leadership is not biblical. Paul described the church as a body, well integrated, with every member working for the good of the whole and for each other. He pleaded to the quarreling Corinthians:

"Now I beseech you, brethren, by the name of our Lord Jesus Christ, that ye all speak the same thing, and that there be no divisions among you; but that ye be perfectly joined together in the same mind and in the same judgment" (1 Cor. 1:10). We cannot always agree, but we are called to develop harmony rather than factions. When divisiveness arises, every faction exercises exclusive power; each excludes others from trust and fellowship as well as office.

The assignment of power in many churches is hurried through with little thought and skimpy prayers. Who holds the power will determine the effectiveness of the church's ministry. Responsibilities must be clearly defined and authority carefully balanced, or abuses will come from the assignment of power.

The Assumption of Power

The assumption of authority within a congregation is not only a *cause* of conflict; it is the very clash of power. Much authority to function within a church is assigned in different ways. However, assumed authority certifies itself. No qualification is necessary. Anyone can surmise that he has the right to direct affairs within his church. Any person may challenge existing authority or presume to speak for others. This is not usually the right thing to do, but it is done. Some people feel God has endowed them with a mandate to tell others what to do. These people assume the power to act.

Assumed power ignores the need to be confirmed by anyone. It presumes to be qualified without being certified. It needs neither credentials nor ability to ascend its dais. Assumed power speaks to others and for others from the sanctions of its own pride.

Our church was emerging from a long power struggle that swirled around staff problems. The battle was over, peace was returning, and we were still intact. Still, a few people hoped to revive dissension. To do this they had to get a hearing before the people.

A member of the church who had no elected office gathered three other men to form a confrontation team. One of the group phoned me Saturday morning and asked me to meet them that afternoon. They wanted to discuss their taking the Sunday morning service for a "vote of confidence discussion." They demanded that I talk without bringing anyone with me. I didn't want to meet them, but there was a gauntlet thrown down! The four were calling me for a capitulation, a shoot-out, or another church fight.

I considered ignoring this call to a meeting. Yet that left the door open for them to make more plans. Also, it might indicate cowardice and a weakening on my part. It frightened me so that I became physically ill. But I went to the meeting, bit the bullet, and covered my fears.

The leader of the group spoke: "Brother Wallace, this church is falling apart, and we are concerned that we'll soon be unable to pay our bills. We can't even proceed with the special project of getting a new bus."

I realized that every crusade for power and change must have a reason. The one church folk seem most sensitive to is financial—not spiritual; money—not righteousness. This group's pretext was financial.

I protested: "The church is paying its bills. Our building indebtedness is down; we've never missed a payment. The value of our land alone is worth over a million dollars. The bank knows that. They have offered us a loan for the bus which the church has already approved. The only reason we don't have a bus is that the committee appointed to purchase it has not functioned."

Another man leaned across the table and jabbed his finger at me before saying: "This church is split right down the middle. They wouldn't decide to buy anything if it were up to them now. We don't have the financial reserve or incentive. We're paralyzed!"

The instigator of the meeting spoke again: "That's the reason we *demand* to bring this to the church tomorrow. I want to impress this situation upon the people and let them decide."

I had noticed that only two of the men spoke; mostly, the man who had assumed leadership. I tried to avoid a direct challenge with him, but it was unavoidable as he felt the momentum building.

"I *demand* that you let me speak to the people from the pulpit in the morning!"

He assumed complete authority for that moment and the next morning's worship hour. He had already spoken in business meeting several times but never prevailed. But a Sunday morning worship congregation was different, especially if the people were caught unaware. The distress and confusion would have been devastating to the spirit now beginning to heal.

The gauntlet again! Graciousness and diplomacy were ignored.

"No, you cannot speak from my pulpit tomorrow. That is the morning worship hour, and it is the domain of the pastor, assigned to him by the congregation. Unless they direct me to do so at a business meeting, I'll not release it."

Outwardly I tried to appear controlled, but inwardly I was almost in panic. I wondered if I'd survive. Then I remembered an axiom from Robert Roark's novel *Something of Value*. The truism was, in effect: "Don't ever take something of pride from a person without giving something of value in return." Such action will concede something to the opposition and strengthen your own position.

I continued, "You seem seriously concerned about the financial stability of our congregation. You also want to buy a bus without an added indebtedness. If that's what this meeting's really about, I'll get the money for you tomorrow."

"How?" the leader demanded incredulously.

"Come to church in the morning, and I'll tell you." The momentum and heat of hostility suddenly waned. I took the occasion to thank them for sharing their concern with me, stood, and dismissed the meeting.

I did not tell anyone of that afternoon's meeting, but Mary and I spent a long time in prayer Saturday night.

At the morning worship hour I told the people of our need for the bus. Also, I mentioned that some members were concerned about adding to the church's indebtedness. I suggested we indicate our willingness to get the bus by pledging some money for it right then.

The appeal turned into an hour-long revival of enthusiasm, with the congregation pledging $5,000 that morning. Many who were absent learned of it and pledged the balance. We paid cash for the bus!

Assumed power may sometimes evolve from an assigned position. An example of this was an elected chairman of a building committee in a church I served during seminary days. He did not really want the educational building to be built. But because of his prominence in the church, he was elected chairman of the building committee. By having this assigned authority, he was able to gain control of the project. It was difficult to call a meeting of the committee against his wishes. When blueprints were finally drawn for the building, he assumed control of them. He would not release them for bids, completely blocking the building for a while. This man assumed the authority to decide what was "best" for the church.

Assumed power must be challenged. Either it should be validated by the people, and so be assigned, or it should be ignored. In most congregationally governed churches, members are reluctant to challenge assumed authority. Such a challenge would normally mean direct confrontation. People with the determination to assume a position of authority learn to confront, so folk usually acquiesce to them. The attitude "everyone has his right as a member" is another reason assumed power is not often contested. Such an outlook on "rights" shows a lack of understanding responsibility.

These negative illustrations are not meant to imply that assumed authority is to be avoided. Sometimes it is necessary. For example: When directives are not clear and action is needed, some power must be assumed.

If the pastor has general oversight of the congregation, there are countless incidents which may occur that are not defined within his assigned authority. In times of crises, he may have to assume certain power; otherwise the church will flounder in debate or be paralyzed by indecision. Every leader must sometimes assume authority. The secret to effective assumption is not to overreach a defensible position. The ability to gauge how much authority a person may assume comes from experience. Such experience often comes from mistakes!

The Absence of Power

The last Monday in March 1981 saw a sudden absence of power at the White House in Washington. President Reagan was shot. Following this assassination attempt there was confusion as to who was in charge. Vice-President Bush was in Texas at the time. Into this vacuum of power men rushed to establish stability. Inevitably there was conflict. Secretary of State Haig stepped nervously to the front declaring, "I am in control here."

This was a dramatic illustration of the absence of power precipitating conflict. In a church or a nation's capitol, when the flow of power to control stops, converging forces often clash. There are many ways an absence of power occurs. In church I have noticed many voids of power occur from (1) an interruption, (2) an abdication, and (3) a deterioration.

The attempt on President Reagan's life brought an interruption to the normal flow of power. Unexpected events interrupt the work of those in authority. A heart attack, a moral collapse, a person absent are examples of other interruptions.

A pastor was accused of an improper relationship with his secretary. There were denials, but obviously he was at least guilty of poor judgment. This interrupted his influence and paralyzed his leadership. Suddenly, in the place of authority, no one was functioning. Into this void of power rushed three competitive groups. The members in leadership positions were challenged by those wanting control. Added to this was a group of young adults who were dissatisfied with the *status quo*. The pastor finally resigned. The young assistant pastor was asked to give temporary leadership to the church. He exercised diplomacy and good judgment. He was accepted by the people and so brought harmony until a new pastor was called.

One summer our church suffered repeated interruptions to its leadership. Several prominent families left the church because of job-related moves from our city. We lost directors from three Sunday School departments, the treasurer of the church, and other vital workers. Fortunately these losses did not leave us in confusion. Our organizations were structured to pass responsibility on in an orderly way.

The absence of power anywhere is a problem. Small areas of responsibility in a church can also cause disruption. A church librarian became seriously ill and was unable to direct her work. Because she hoped to recover her health and return, she did not resign. But she did not return quickly. No one with authority moved to provide temporary help in the library. Differences of opinion were expressed as to what should be done. When nothing was done, small disputes brought hurt feelings which ballooned into serious controversy. Soon angry people quarreled over matters not related to the library problem. The interruption of even limited power can bring discord.

The abdication of power is a common occurrence; it simply is the giving up of authority. *Resigning* a position is one form of abdication.

Sometimes conflict explodes over the very fact of a resignation—over whether or not it should be done.

We have a long-standing policy in our church that we do not vote on a resignation. If a person resigns we accept that person's decision as being sincere and intelligent. This keeps resignations from drawing people into disputes over reasons they do not wish to address directly or openly. It also avoids placing the blame of a resignation on someone other than the person making it.

Abdications also occur indirectly—for example, when a person refuses to fulfill his responsibility of leadership, yet will not resign that office. Simply not doing what should be done is a form of abdication. It leaves a vacuum for criticism and conflict to fill.

A director of training watched the interest in Christian training die. Yet he refused to make any changes. He would not organize a council and refused to consider new plans. He was adamantly opposed to reorganization of the training department.

"What are you going to do, Claude?" he was asked.

"I'm not going to do anything differently. What we're doing is good enough."

Claude abdicated his leadership without giving up his office. This meant an absence of power—so came conflict!

My own feeling dictates that it is better to have no one in a position than to have someone who will not function. In either case power is absent; but in the latter, an obstacle blocks progress.

Many churches have a system of rotating membership on boards and committees. Those that do not hazard an indirect abdication of power.

The manner of abdication is crucial. A person can resign in such a way as to create chaos.

Eddie Crowe was engaged as the director of Christian ministries at the Baywater Church. Specific responsibilities were described in his job contract. His supervisor on the staff was assigned. Expectations as to his on-the-job training were agreed upon. Eddie signed the contract along with the director of personnel.

Within a year Eddie resigned his position by writing a letter to the board of elders rather than to his supervisor. Before he sent the letter to the board, he "leaked" his reasons for leaving to influential friends in the congregation. In his resignation he blamed the pastor for not permitting him to "follow the leading of the Holy Spirit." Eddie proposed that he be allowed to serve "as God directs" rather than from the job description. He contrived the image of a servant of God who was denied freedom to work.

This resignation had its desired effect; accusations and divisiveness swirled while Eddie stood aside with an air of grieved innocence. The *manner* of the resignation stirred conflict, rather than the fact itself.

In contrast, a famous abdication was made by a direct statement. Edward VIII, King of England, resigned in the year 1936. On December 11 of that same year he abdicated because he wanted to marry Mrs. Wallis Warfield Simpson, a twice-divorced American woman. The British government did not feel that this was in keeping with the Crown's tradition and dignity. Edward therefore abdicated by making a simple speech on the radio. He said, in effect, "I cannot continue as king without the woman I love by my side." Without rancor or blame he assumed the responsibility for his choice to abdicate. He demonstrated nobility in his manner.

Everybody has to quit sometimes. Changes must come. But the way we lay down power and depart our place shows our character. Even under duress, amid difficulties, nobility is expected of the king's family—and such we are. A wise and gracious resignation prepares for a smooth transition of power.

Another way power is lost is by *deterioration*. This is what I dread the most. I fear it because it occurs so subtly. Power can be lost so slowly as to be imperceptible. It atrophies like a muscle unused. It drifts away like an outgoing tide. It fades like color in the sun. And when it's gone there is an emptiness other forces fill.

I've seen the deterioration of power through inactivity, through intransigence, and through indifference. In these three ways, churches and persons lose power. With this loss of power, strife often invades the church.

Inactivity causes a deterioration of power. "If you don't use it, you'll lose it" is true of power. If a person has a responsibility, he has the potential of power to do the job. Or at least that should be so. Responsibility should always be accompanied by authority. If there is no action which demands power, things don't stay the same; they deteriorate.

Personal or spiritual power is similar to physical power in that it develops only as used. Like a muscle, strength grows as exercised, but deteriorates if unused. Inactivity of any sort brings the subsiding of power.

Power also deteriorates through *intransigence*. At times contending groups in a church refuse to compromise their differences. Often such disagreements cannot be resolved by a simple win/lose vote. When the attitude of people becomes locked into an adamant hostility, the church degenerates.

Our church was once gripped in a deadlock of disagreements. One group was determined to make a change in the entire leadership. The other side was just as unyielding in a *status quo* position. I felt the coldness in our worship. I experienced a helplessness in persuasion. Communication between the two factions was meaningless.

Nothing functioned with any dynamic. We moved through our church activities like figures in a dream, unrelated to each other. It was obvious that other facets of our church would soon deteriorate—numbers, offerings, activities, everything. We were like two wrestlers locked into desperate holds where neither dared make a new move lest the other get an advantage. Yet there had to be a change!

To make a move toward that change I recommended to the deacons that the church engage a psychologist, skilled in personal counseling. He would spend a certain number of hours each week at the church, for a few months. His purpose would be to have a personal, confidential interview with members of our church. His primary responsibility would be to talk with leaders of the church—officers, teachers, committee persons. Other members who wished to talk with him would also be heard. He would try to persuade them to voice their feelings and attitudes about the church. He was pledged to confidentiality about who said what. He would report to the pastor each week and to the deacons monthly. He would give his impressions as to what the grievances were and how they might be handled. However, we were not bound to implement his suggestions for change.

When I presented this idea to the deacons, they were very reluctant to recommend it. They had never heard of such a tactic before; neither had I. They were afraid of how the people might react. So was I! But no one had any other suggestion for a resolution of our deadlock. They did recommend it to the church, and it was approved.

The psychologist came and interviewed many people. Some invited to talk did not respond. There was no criticism of who met with him, or who did not. The main purpose of the plan worked in that it gave people an opportunity to vent their feelings without fear of retaliation. It also revealed to me and to the deacons some feelings of which we were unaware. We saw places we could make changes. Some things did not change, but there was movement and flexing of attitudes. We began to grant one another the right to have feelings that differed, although the facts remained the same.

I learned that sometimes reconciliations cannot begin by simply dealing with the *facts* in a matter. We often must begin first to deal with the feelings which color those facts. Feelings must be recognized, even if not agreed with. Then there can be freedom for each adversary to move from his intransigence.

Personal feelings are infinitely complex, formed from the myriad of experiences unique to each individual. This is what often blocks our relationships; we want the other person to feel the same way about a matter that we do. Often that's impossible because of vastly different background experiences. But when we are allowed to hold our feelings, we have more freedom to deal with facts. Without some liberty to express our feelings, we often remain adamant.

The final way I have seen the deterioration of power is through *indifference*. That is an attitude of not caring about a responsibility. Indifference ignores God's will as it attends its own desires.

I have drifted into periods of indifference when I went through religious rituals with no enthusiasm. I've said prayers without feeling and proclaimed truths without conviction. The danger of such indifference is that it erodes power imperceptibly.

Samson illustrates such a loss of power through indifference. He flirted repeatedly with Delilah, indifferent to what God warned. One time he awoke in Delilah's lap, stretched himself as before, but did not know his power was gone. But the Philistines knew! They always do recognize the absence of power—then comes conflict and defeat.

The absence of power opens the gates to trouble just as does the abuse of power. Weakness is as dangerous as wickedness. The assumption of power may be wrong, and in the assignment of power there may be mistakes. But the absence of power leaves a church without any defense in all these avenues to conflict.

6

Conduct in Conflict

In the midst of church fights I have heard people say, "Why do Christians behave like that?" When "good" church members act like calloused people of the world, we wonder why. We presume that within the circle of church life, each member will behave ideally.

We read the Bible; we teach it and hear it preached. Yet we often fail to live what we learn. Much of the New Testament was written to persuade church members not to live as they had before. Listen to these interesting instructions from the apostle Paul to the Christians in Ephesus:

> So I tell you this, and insist on it in the Lord, that you must no longer live as the Gentiles do, . . . They are darkened in their understanding and separated from the life of God . . . You, however, did not come to know Christ that way. . . . You were taught, with regard to your former way of life, to put off your old self, which is being corrupted by its deceitful desires; to be made new in the attitude of your minds; . . . Therefore each of you must put off falsehood and speak truthfully to his neighbor, . . . In your anger do not sin . . . and do not give the devil a foothold. . . . Do not let any unwholesome talk come out of your mouths, but only what is helpful for building others up according to their needs, that it may benefit those who listen. . . . Get rid of all bitterness, rage and anger, brawling and slander, along with every form of malice. Be kind and compassionate to one another, forgiving each other, just as in Christ God forgave you (Eph. 4:17-32, NIV).

Understanding Our Actions

Sometimes we as Christians don't understand why we act as we do. But this insight would improve our own behavior and give us wisdom in dealing with others. Three perspectives can bring us insight into why we act as we do: historically, we are influenced by our own personal background; socially, we are affected by the society in which we live; spiritually, we are controlled by the spirit that dominates our actions.

Historical Influences. Historically, we live as we have learned to live. The way we relate to other people is a learned process. Our ability to communicate feelings and desires has its roots in our background. The way a family handles its crises demonstrates for the children how they will respond to problems. Some families fight over their differences. Words are their weapons, and deviousness is their strategy of attack. Others suppress their anger rather than vent it. Then resentment simmers while relationships deteriorate. Other families practice direct communication. They develop understanding and resolve their differences. When people come into the church family, they generally continue to use the same patterns of relationships they have already learned.

Another part of historical influence upon people is their church experiences. The churches they have belonged to demonstrated a certain behavior. Bill is a good example of this principle. He was a member of a prominent family in the church at Tinkertown. Pastors did not stay long at Tinkertown. The pay was small and criticism abundant. "Roast preacher" was served at Bill's family dinner table every Sunday.

Bill went to church business meetings with the family. His father usually took issue over something. Differences were then settled by heated debates that left everyone upset. No one seemed to know of a better way to get things done.

Bill grew up, married, moved to another town, and joined a church. How was he to act in this new church? He knew only one way—"the way we did it back home." Bill's wife had a different background. Members of her family were nonconfronting in their relationships. If they felt ill at ease over differences, they just left the church. Bill's new family developed a combination from those two backgrounds. Bill was always vocal and negative in his church. His family periodically withdrew from active church life. Eventually they moved their membership to another congregation, only to repeat the same behavior pattern. People behave as they do because of historical influences in their lives.

Social Influences. Another strong influence in church conduct is social in nature. Theoretically, the church is "separate from the world." We are in the world, and the world is not supposed to be in the church. But it is. When people come to church they bring the feelings that have dominated their environment. They don't usually leave their tensions at home. Problems seldom are locked away at the office. Emotions we have repressed elsewhere often find vent at church.

During a turbulent deacons' meeting, I wondered why there was so much contention over trivia. Most of the discord seemed to come from one man. That night he took issue with everything involving finances.

After the meeting I approached him in private. "Is there anything wrong, Derrick? You were so intense about things which didn't seem terribly important."

"My wife has really messed us up financially. She made another bad buy today, and we went deeper into debt. I've talked with her, but it doesn't do any good. I'm frustrated and angry. Maybe that's what caused my explosion tonight."

So many harsh emotions generated outside the church are brought in and discharged. We presume that other people will have a "Christian spirit" within the church and not retaliate. I confronted a deacon one time about his continual verbal abuse of me. "Don't you feel that as an influential Christian you should treat me in a Christian manner?"

"But you are supposed to be a better Christian than I am. You should take it, even if I don't do right."

All kinds of bad emotions are transferred into the church from outside experiences. It's a dumping ground for resentments and frustrations. To understand this doesn't make it right; nor does seeing it solve the problem. But, if we perceive the influence at work, it may help us avoid a serious clash of emotions.

Social influences also invade the church indirectly through world events and behavior trends. The rebellion against "the establishment" during the sixties hurt the church. A decline in attendance was accompanied by an exodus from pew and pulpit. Many disturbing incidents at church were energized by the turbulence within society.

In the past twenty years there has been a proliferation of activist groups. Anyone who wants to protest authority can generate support. Parents organize to change the rules at school. Children sue parents. Convicted felons claim constitutional rights. Illegal aliens demand privileges from our government. The spirit of protest and extreme individualism pervades society. It also invades the church.

Spiritual Influences. A Wednesday night business meeting of our congregation concluded several months of strife. It was an unpleasant session followed by angry groups in the parking lot giving vent to ugly feelings.

The following Sunday morning I felt moved to do something I'd never done before—talk about the business meeting at a worship service. That message quieted and stabilized the mood of our people. Among my comments was a statement that startled some: "This disagreement among us has been a very spiritual experience. It has revealed our spirit, individually and as a church. It has indeed been a deeply spiritual encounter."

Normally we use the expression *spiritual* to indicate some good action controlled by the Holy Spirit. This is a theological and limited use of the word. Because man is spirit, his actions originate with his "spirit." We act as we do because of history's influence behind us and society's pressure around us. We also behave according to the character of our own inner spirit.

Our spirit within may be described as a flowing stream. Our spirit is always gathering from life's tributaries other forces and elements which affect the character of its flow.

The Holy Spirit enters our life like a new tributary pouring into our spirit flow. His coming does not remove the original nature of our life, but pervades it with new force. Unfortunately, the Holy Spirit may be choked to a trickle by other elements that dominate our spirit flow.

Most of us seldom examine our spirit flow. We just presume that the other person's spirit is always the one that's polluted and turbulent. We are reluctant to probe our own spirit for the strong forces that affect our actions.

The influences that pour through our spirit flow are many and deep. These inner forces motivate our conduct. We must recognize their influence if we are to control our conduct. Many times we refuse to consider our feelings. We are sometimes like a church staff member with whom I worked for a while. He and I were in conference about controversial matters. I was agitated by his indolence and failure to do necessary tasks of ministry. When I did not try to hide my feelings, he said in sweet rebuke, "Brother Wallace, the Lord has given me victory over anger and pride. You need to pray for such deliverance."

That did it! I broke into laughter. Never had I known a person more proud of his "spirituality" than he. He had a great deal of anger, but he managed to suppress it. Numerous times he had told members of the church half-truths, manipulating them to express his anger at the pastor.

This person denied the elements in his spirit which he didn't like. He preferred to believe the Holy Spirit motivated *all* his deeds. He never dealt with the forces that troubled him.

When I try to understand what forces influence me, four questions help: (1) What do I believe? (2) What do I want? (3) What do I love? (4) What do I fear?

1. *Belief.* Belief is basic to life. Yet it is one of the most misunderstood and misused words. New Testament belief pertains more to dynamic than dogma, more to conduct than creed. Belief is the concave, and action is the convex of life's circumference. What is believed inwardly is shown outwardly. "Faith without works is dead" is another way of saying, "If you don't do it, you don't believe it." Or turn the meaning around: "What we believe, that we do." When we act a certain way, it is backed by belief about the causes and consequences of our deed. People would not behave in certain unscrupulous ways if they believed what the Bible says about God and judgment. If we really believed what the Bible says about kindness, generosity, and forgiveness, there would be more reconciliation in the church. What do we really believe about the way we behave?

2. *Desire.* "What do you *want* me to do?" "Do you *want* to get

well?" were questions Jesus asked people. Jesus also made offers to people: "Come follow me." Peter followed, but the rich young ruler did not; their desires were different. What we really want is often disguised. We may deny some desires because we feel they are wrong; nevertheless, they are always there, pressuring us in certain directions.

It's not wrong to have desires, but sometimes desire is tainted by envy. Envy does not simply want something for itself; it wishes less for others. An envious person will block someone from a responsibility in the church not because he wants it for himself, but because he wishes ill for that person. "What is it that I really want which is being expressed by my behavior?" This is one of the most important questions we can ask ourselves.

3. *Love*. The dominant motive for our behavior should be love. In the church we use this word carelessly. We profess love for one another, then treat each other with indifference and shocking insensitivity. We claim to love, yet we don't consider how our words and deeds may affect a person. We don't bother to find out how they feel or think when there's a disagreement. We read 1 Corinthians 13, yet we don't use it to measure our conduct. We should love one another, but our behavior too often reflects self-love and love for the wrong things.

Early in my ministry a man came to my office. He prefaced his comments by saying: "Pastor, I love you, but. . . . " Then he proceeded to give me a tongue-lashing that still makes me wince every time I hear, "I love you, but. . . . " I don't remember a thing he talked about, but I haven't forgotten his spirit. He never asked me one question about my feelings or thoughts. He didn't offer me an opportunity to respond. He finished his tirade, then turned and walked out.

Love can become angry—and it should under some circumstances. But love must control the intensity and purpose of anger's expression. Our love for one another should be evident by our deeds as well as our words. We may get into controversy because our love for Jesus calls us to the challenge. However, we need to be careful to keep his commandments while we struggle.

4. *Fear*. The emotion of fear is usually a greater motivator than love for most of us. The places and emphases of fear in the Scriptures

are startling. In the Bible, fear is the first emotion that man is said to have experienced (Gen. 3:10). Fear is mentioned in the Scriptures long before love. The Old Testament began with the presence of fear, and Malachi closed the ancient Book with the mention of fear.

The New Testament opens with the life of Jesus bracketed by this same dark emotion: "Now the birth of Jesus Christ was on this wise: . . . behold, the angel of the Lord appeared unto him [Joseph] in a dream, saying, . . . fear not to take unto thee Mary thy wife" (Matt. 1:18-20). An angel said to the women on that resurrection morning, "Fear not . . . " Then Jesus met them and said, "Be not afraid . . . " (Matt. 28:5,10). Near the close of the Word of God, those who are characterized by fear are warned (Rev. 21:8). Fear is such a tyrant over humanity that both in the Old and New Testaments God repeatedly encourages us by saying, "Fear not . . . be not afraid. . . . "

Yet we let fear drive us to irrational behavior or paralyze reasonable actions. In my own life fear has been painfully present in many confrontations. Then that fear has often given me my greatest intensity. I want love and faith to dominate my life, but still I know that fear infects much of my spirit. I have traced many of my fears to my experiences in childhood and youth. That helps me understand and conquer them—but not entirely.

As I've watched people in the church react to disagreements, I believe that fear is the most frequent stimulus to controversy. They are afraid that they will be rejected, ignored, or replaced. They fear that they'll be quoted or misquoted. People fear that someone will get an advantage they don't have or a recognition they've not attained. Many of us tremble at the thought of our true selves being discovered. We are in anguish that our power will be taken, a cherished position usurped, or some inadequacy revealed. So we stir up an angry storm of controversy to camouflage what we really fear.

Anger in the church is prompted by fear more often than by righteousness. Fear touches our lives at every level. Many times fear is the source of other negative emotions, especially anger.

Because we trust so poorly, we fear strongly. Again and again Jesus pleads with his followers not to be afraid. He tries to reassure them there is nothing to fear if they trust him. He repeatedly sets faith and fear in diametric contrast. "Let not your heart be troubled:

ye believe in God, believe also in me. . . . Peace I leave with you, . . . Let not your heart be troubled, neither let it be afraid" (John 14:1,27).

Guidelines for Conduct in Conflict

It is essential that we understand influences which affect our conduct. But knowing is not enough. We can know why we do something wrong and still continue in it. Through the years I have developed a few simple guidelines for my own conduct in conflict. These are certainly not comprehensive for every complex situation, but they can help us keep control of ourselves in confrontations.

Don't Lose Control of Your Emotions! Control of emotions does not mean we are emotionless. True feelings may be evident, but we must not turn our behavior over to our emotions. Emotions without restraint tend to balloon. They are like wind and fire—effective under control but destructive when released.

There are many ways we let emotions dominate our behavior. One way occurs when we threaten another person. By using threat we try to influence through fear. "We're thinking about leaving the church. . . ." "We wouldn't want to put your little family out in the street. . . ." "If you vote with that bunch, I'll have to refuse you further credit. . . ."

Threats are despised everywhere, but threats are especially out of place in the life of a Christian. It was said of Jesus that "he threatened not" (1 Pet. 2:23). Paul admonished Christians to stop using threats (Eph. 6:9). We must beware, lest using threats on others we find ourselves behaving like enemies of Jesus (Acts 4:17,21,29; 9:1).

Anger gets out of control easily. Paul said, "Be ye angry, and sin not" (Eph. 4:26). That's a rare feat. For a leader, anger often becomes a trap. If a person can be made to flash with anger, he may lose control and do something wrong. Then his behavior self-destructs.

Losing our temper is not always expressed by vocal outburst or violent acts. Sometimes anger burns silently. My family lived in a parsonage for eighteen years. The church had told us that rent-free housing was part of our salary. The leaders of the church eventually came to realize that they had not provided their pastor with basic security over the years. My family had no equity in a home and little security for the years ahead. So these thoughtful leaders proposed to give me the parsonage. This stirred envy and anger in some of the members.

These angry members came to the church business meeting. When the proposal was made and discussion was called for, no one spoke. Not a question was asked. No inquiries were made into the reason or background of that generous offer. Intense anger was evident on many faces, but no one spoke. They did not care to consider; they came only to express their anger with a negative vote. The silent indifference hurt almost as much as their negative vote.

Another subtle way emotions can take control is demonstrated through our sulking and pouting. Some people put on a sad countenance "that they may be seen of men." By this they hope to generate sympathy. Honest emotions merit Christian sympathy, but some grief should be carried before the Lord alone. Some Christians advertise their "spirituality" by facial expressions akin to stomach distress. Jesus warned his disciples against such display.

"When you fast, do not look somber as the hypocrites do, for they disfigure their faces to show men they are fasting. . . . But when you fast, put oil on your head and wash your face, so that it will not be obvious to men that you are fasting, but only to your Father, who is unseen" (Matt. 6:16-18, NIV).

The Lord taught that we should wear a good countenance before the world. Whether we come from fasting or a fuss, we should control our emotions and display a pleasant appearance.

Name-calling and gossip are also undisciplined emotional expressions. Conflict is often highly emotional. Feelings are inseparable from life, but we must not openly lose emotional control in the heat of contention.

Don't Deceive. One of the first inclinations when differences arise between persons is to deceive. Nothing destroys like deceit. On the other hand, nothing strengthens like integrity. Peter wrote of Jesus: "Who did no sin, neither was guile found in his mouth" (1 Pet. 2:22). The most basic element in our relationship to God and to each other is trust. If we cannot believe in a person, we will never establish a significant relationship with him.

Barclay's translation of John 2:23 emphasizes this in the life of Jesus. "When he was in Jerusalem, at the Passover, at the Feast, many believed in his name, as they saw the signs which he did; but Jesus himself would not entrust himself to them, because he knew them all, and because he had no need that anyone should testify to him what man is like, for he well knew what was in human nature."[1] Those people believed only in what they saw. Jesus wanted a different kind of faith from them. So he did not entrust himself to them. No relationship was formed because deep trust was absent.

Trust is not extended automatically in a personal contact. We may wish it were so, but only tenuous trust is extended at first in a relationship. Then as it is justified we slowly build confidence. If trust in our integrity is lost, it is hard to regain.

Some of the compliments I cherish most have come from my "sometimes enemies." In a vicious and dragged-out church fight, we engaged a psychologist to observe the situation and be available to our people. At a report session the psychologist commented with surprise: "John, some of your opponents say they hate your guts, but they trust you. They believe you're trying to do what you think is best for the church." From that thread of trust we eventually were able to weave a new relationship with some alienated members. Sometimes integrity is all we have to hang on to.

Don't Presume. I often pray David's prayer: "Keep back thy servant also from presumptuous sins; let them not have dominion over me: then I shall be upright, and I shall be innocent from the great transgression" (Ps. 19:18).

We presume too much! We presume we are right without examining a matter thoroughly. We presume the "other side" in a conflict is of the devil. We presume we have communicated clearly. We presume if people are quiet, everything's all right. We presume if we ignore a wrong, it will go away. We presume that to say something is to do it. We presume that our opposition's enemy is our friend. We presume that *our* point of view is understood and *our* good motives are obvious. We presume that a "real Christian" will see things as we do.

Then there's that dangerous presumption: You can trust a person because he talks in religious terms. Early in my ministry there was a power struggle in our church. Attempts were made to discredit my leadership and have me removed as pastor. But they failed. The church was growing, and we had bought attractive new property to which we would eventually move the congregation.

Late one winter night a phone call came to the parsonage. A young woman's voice pleaded, "I need your help."

"What kind of help?" I asked.

"I need some spiritual advice."

"Who are you, and why did you call *me*?"

She gave me a name and explained, "I just looked in the phone book and picked out your name. Would you come talk to me?"

"We can talk over the phone."

"No, the people here don't like me to borrow their phone."

"I can see you at your home or at the church in the morning; that's only a few hours away."

"No, I need to talk now," she pleaded repeatedly.

I agreed to come. She told me where she rented a back bedroom in an old house near our church.

"I know where the house is. You turn on the fire and a light in the front living room, and I'll talk with you there."

Although she sounded convincing, I was apprehensive. My wife could not accompany me because our three small children could not be left alone. I picked up the phone and called a deacon who was also on the city police force. "Bill, I want you to make a pastoral call with me."

"You mean, *now*?" he answered sleepily.

"Yes, I'll be over in about fifteen minutes. We're going down on Big Tree Lane."

We drove down the long, dark block. The house, about midway, was back in the shadows. No lights were on. We walked up on the porch and knocked. The young lady came to the door without turning on any lights. When she opened the door, I could see through the darkened house to a dim light in a small, back room.

"I'm John Wallace. You phoned me to come talk with you. But there's no fire and light in this front room."

"The people here don't like me burning lights and gas in any room but the one I rent. You can come back to my room, and we'll talk."

Bill was standing in the shadows on the dark porch. "Bill, you come with us. Miss, this is a deacon from our church. He came to visit with me."

Bill stepped forward. She was startled; she stood looking at us, perplexed. Then she turned and walked back to her room. One straight chair, a tiny dresser, and a double bed crowded the dingy room. At the foot of the bed was a closet with an old curtain draped across the opening. Bill stepped to the closet and stood with his back to the curtain. The girl sat on the bed while I took the rickety chair.

"Now what is it that's troubling you this late at night?" I inquired.

"Well, I just got to wondering, and I can't understand where Cain got his wife."

There was a long silence. Bill smiled and shifted his big shoulder against the wall. Not a sound in the house. The girl did seem distressed, but somehow her distress lacked spiritual authenticity. I gave her an explanation to the Genesis history of Cain, then invited her to a Sunday School class at our church.

Years later when I confronted a man about the incident, he told me enough to confirm the obvious setup. They didn't count on my bringing someone along for the visit. I learned early in my ministry not to presume.

Don't Retaliate. Every reasonable person abhors terrorism. But terrorism is retaliation's ultimate expression. Terrorism is the monster that grows from an uncontrolled desire for revenge. Jesus warned against that natural reaction of returning evil for evil, an eye for an eye, and a hurt for a hurt.

The vengeful spirit among the children of God is an alien spirit. Yet, because vindictiveness is so much a part of our human nature, we retaliate almost by reflex.

Retaliation continues a conflict. It's a crosscut saw with two parties pulling back and forth while they cut down spiritual growth that has taken years to develop.

Retribution's evil spirit ignores the warning of Jesus that we must forgive our brother, if God is to forgive us (Matt. 6:14-15; 18:35). We sometimes go through the motions of reconciliation without changing our attitude. There is one sure sign of genuine reconciliation: the presence of joy and gladness. When there's no joy in a relationship that has supposedly been mended, usually bits of resentment remain. When the father and his prodigal son were reconciled, rejoicing broke out. When a sinner returns to the Heavenly Father, angels rejoice (Luke 15:7). When we abandon the desire for revenge and embrace reconciliation, gladness sings in our hearts. We are deprived of both forgiveness and joy if we want to avenge a wrong.

The desire for revenge destroys the person who holds it. It is a slow, emotional cancer eating away at peace and happiness. A bitter spirit-flow poisons the person through which it moves. An acerbic spirit contributes to stomach ulcers and other ills of the body, to say nothing of etching harsh lines in the face. In our obsession for revenge, the hurt we would do another we always wreak upon ourselves.

Nothing is more destructive to reconciliation than the attitude that we have a right to avenge a hurt done to us. I have known men to stand outside the sanctuary and say to incoming worshipers, "Be here Wednesday night, and we'll get 'em this time!" We have all heard, "I'll get even with you if it's the last thing I do," and "You can't talk to me like that and get away with it."

In the thirty-two years I have been pastor of this congregation, some people have left the church in anger. In time, a number have returned and experienced reconciliation. Some who have not joined our church have asked me personally for help in crises. There would have been no healing of broken relationships if I or our church members had threatened retaliation. An attitude of retribution on our part would have walled off their return.

Retaliation is an act of disobedience to God. One of the most profound writings on Christian conduct is Paul's twelfth chapter in Romans. Repeatedly he warns against retribution. His concluding emphasis is, "Do not take revenge, my friends, but leave room for God's wrath, for it is written: 'It is mine to avenge; I will repay,' says the Lord" (Rom. 12:19, NIV).

At the threshold of my ministerial education a religious leader said, in effect, "John, if you don't quit disagreeing with me, I'll never be able to recommend you to any position in the ministry." And he never did. Several opportunities which came my way were denied me by his influence. I wonder how he reconciled his attitude with Romans 12.

It's natural to react with a certain vengeance when we've been hurt. When revenge fantasies flash upon my mind, I forcefully shut them off. Then I turn my spirit to obey God, whether I feel like it or not. "'It is *mine* to avenge; I will repay,' says the Lord. . . . Do not be overcome by evil, but overcome evil with good" (Rom. 12:19*b*,21, NIV).

Along with the several negatives I try to avoid in conflict, certain positive things to *do* are also essential. These actions have helped me avoid catastrophe at times.

Evaluation. Most of us slide into controversy before we realize it. Forces and differences trap us in disagreement. Then we feel there is nothing to do but back off or fight. There are other constructive alternatives.

When a divisive contest begins to develop, I try to pause and evaluate. I take a careful look at what is happening in the dynamics of human relationship.

The first evaluation for me is the *why* of this discord. Is it over feelings or principles? What are the strong motivators of the struggle? Are there hidden causes for disagreements?

Sam was pastor of a small village congregation. The church had never been financially strong. After a year as pastor, Sam was approached by one of the deacons and told he should resign because of the poor condition of the church finances. The truth was that other pastors had served there with less money coming in. The big difference was that the former pastor had always gone to this deacon and discussed his ideas before telling the church. But this young pastor had not checked his leadership goals with him. The man resented being ignored and felt his power over the church slipping away. So he used money to camouflage his motive in attacking Sam's threat to his ego.

Some reasons for conflict are clear-cut and evident. But most have complex dynamics. It is good to be aware of these factors even if we can't change them.

Closely associated with an evaluation of the why of controversy is the *who* of it. Sometimes the *who* reveals the *why*. Some people are always contentious, controversial, and caustic!

Other people may be counted upon to become involved in conflicts of principle. They are people of noble convictions, and their attitudes need to be reckoned with.

Some church members must not be ignored, whether they are agreed with or not. They should be listened to and their reasoning weighed. Ernest was one of the most respected men in our church.

He was quiet and reserved, yet strong and fearless when confronting opposition. I talked to him about a decision I was planning to make. This choice was controversial. He advised me against it, yet did not withdraw his friendship when I proceeded against his mature judgment. A few weeks later I found myself wishing I had listened to Ernest!

The *who* of a conflict will often indicate what kind of strife may develop. Many people are predictable. Always evaluate who is active in a struggle. That's hard to do if you've never known that person in conflict. "You never know a person until you know him in conflict" is a favorite axiom of mine.

Another essential evaluation is the worth of conflict's goal. All disagreements do not have equal significance. Some hardly matter, while others have tremendous consequences at stake. Will the escalation of the conflict be worth what the contention costs? A lot of quarrels are simply not worth their emotional effort. People who have to win every argument and fight to the bitter end pay a high price for trivia.

Will the gain be worth the price of the controversy? What will it cost in human relationships to wage the battle? What might it cost to *lose* the dispute? Will it be simply a loss of face or a loss of place?

I knew a pastor who had a disagreement with a deacon over a gallon of paint for the parsonage kitchen. The contention became a "shoot-out," and the preacher lost his job—over one bucket of cheap paint!

If you decide to continue in the controversy, evaluate the cost in time, effort, and resources. If the dissension becomes churchwide, what will it cost the church? What will the price be emotionally, physically, and financially? But don't ignore this question: "What will be the loss if I do *not* continue the struggle?"

Is it possible that with proper behavior, you could win more by losing? Taking a loss in the proper spirit has its advantages. Or would you ultimately lose more by winning that dispute?

Take an inventory of your resources for whatever type of conflict you face. What is your knowledge of the matter? What financial resources will you need? Who will support you, or can you stand alone? Is truth and dignity on your side? What are your emotional strengths? Are your communication skills limited primarily to volume? What kinds of power will you need to make the right things happen? Do you have access to resources you may not now have? Do you have the temperament for this challenge?

If you cannot answer many evaluation questions with some encouraging certainty, back off; think it over and pray about it. The unknown usually hides the unexpected.

Communication. "In the beginning was the Word, . . . and the Word was God" (John 1:1). In the Scriptures God is described by many analogies. But this most significant description uses a term of communication. In Jesus Christ, God communicated himself through a perfect human life and called that life "the Word." One characteristic of God is his communicative nature. Yet his followers are woefully unlike God in their inability to communicate with one another.

Conflicts are seldom resolved happily because we communicate so poorly. There is no denying that a great deal of communication goes on in the average congregation. We convey feelings and attitudes to one another by many nonverbal signals. When conflicts arise, we tend to stop talking to our opponents and convey our frame of mind by nonverbal signals. But nonverbal signals are not adequate to resolve disagreements. We must use the power of words to develop understanding and resolve differences. If we refuse to sit down and talk, there is no other way of reconciling.

The Scriptures emphasize communication with the spoken word. "Come now, let us reason together, saith the Lord" (Isa. 1:18). "If we confess our sins" (1 John 1:9). "Confess your faults one to another" (Jas. 5:16). "if thy brother shall trespass against thee, go and tell him his fault . . . if he shall hear thee, . . . if he shall neglect to hear them, tell it unto the church:" (Matt. 18:17). "Be ready always to give an answer" (1 Pet. 3:15). "Let every man be swift to hear" (Jas. 1:19). The Bible teaches that differences should be resolved by mutual, verbal interchange of honest attitudes.

The problems of communication in a church conflict are difficult because all relationships are voluntary. People don't have to talk or listen unless they want to. In addition to this, most church meetings are structured away from dialogue.

For me, three elements are basic to effective conflict communication: (1) articulation, (2) information, and (3) concentration. In the church we are usually weak in all three.

1. *Articulation.* In church controversies we fail to articulate our disagreements. We radiate our displeasure but do not voice it. We manipulate our anger but do not admit it. We suppress our hostility and feel pious about not causing trouble, but it burns deep within us and breaks out years later in harmful ways.

We behave like this at church because it is our pattern everywhere else. Martin Buber once said, "A person's inability to carry on authentic dialogue with one another is the most acute symptom of the pathology of our time."[2] We must articulate our feelings and thoughts in a conflict.

We need to plan the situation which will permit the most effective communication. Ask for a meeting with the alienated person. Structure the time and place. The lighting in a room, its furnishings, the seating of individuals—all are important for conversation. Do not fail to give attention to the ventilation and temperature of the place. Fresh air and low temperature sharpens our minds—and makes humor easier. Stale air and high temperature irritate and dull us. Parenthetically, a congregational business meeting is a poor place to resolve differences. Large groups don't dialogue; they polarize. But if that's the only place people will talk, structure the discussion—and talk!

Speak your honest feelings. Many times people do not talk about what really troubles them. Years after some incidents, I've learned that people have been hurt and angry for a long time. The reasons for our silence are many—pride, shame, fear, frustration, anger, cynicism, ignorance, distrust. All these repress our inclination to talk.

I've found talking to be like writing in this respect: Just get at it until it's done. Don't wait until you feel like talking; plan to talk and do it! Your expressions may not be polished, but dialogue will refine our understanding. This prepares for reconciliation.

Sometimes a counselor-referee is needed in a confrontation. Churches are reluctant to engage such a helper. "It seems Christians ought to be able to work out their problems without a stranger involved." I hear that in both church and marriage conflicts. The result is that conflicting sides are not able to work out their problems.

A counselor can guide and instruct in the process of communication without taking sides. We fail in everything from the family to international affairs because we do not learn to talk together.

I made a pastoral call on a man who had been absent from church for a long time. I used two questions that threw open the door of relationship the best I knew, especially when I didn't know anything else to say: "Is there anything you'd like the church or me to do?" "Is there anything you'd like to ask me or tell me?"

"Yes, there is!"

"Please do."

"You let me down in a church controversy with some other members five years ago. I've been mad at you and the church ever since. Now, I want to tell you how I feel."

With deep emotion he talked for an hour. I felt nothing but sadness that he'd carried this burning in his spirit all these years. Just holding it in had isolated him from friends. It probably was a factor in his ill health.

"Meyer, why didn't you tell me before now? I called on you and the others to talk it over then. You implied everything was all right."

"I don't know—I just didn't."

When we are in disagreements we should try to articulate it. Say it, spell it out, cry it out; be sure what should be said is verbalized. But remain in control; be sure what shouldn't be said remains inside.

2. *Information.* Too often we try to settle problems without enough information. When we discuss our differences, let's get the facts. This means careful records need to be kept in church matters. When I had to explain the firing of a staff member, the dismissed person sought defense behind a storm of emotion. I read a summary of numerous staff meetings and his delinquent work record. When the people heard those specifics, they supported the dismissal.

Hours are wasted in committee arguments over matters that could be settled if specific information were available. Instead, the committee generates antagonism with, "I think," "I knew a friend that," "Well, I heard," "It seems to me," "What if."

Many people prefer to speak in nonspecifics. They do not want to communicate with facts. Ambiguity permits evasion of responsibility. If peace and order are to prevail, we must talk in specifics. Records sometimes seem a waste of effort. But in a crisis, exact information can save time and effort.

At a deacons' meeting, two men were irritated with what they felt was the improper handling of a resignation. This had been voluntarily communicated to me by the staff person involved. I accepted the resignation, then asked the staff member to give it to me in writing. I did not argue with the deacons; I just handed them the letter to read. There was no further complaint. If we had tried to settle their objections with "I said," "they said," "she said," it would never have been resolved.

3. *Concentration.* Talking is necessary; facts are essential; but without attentive listening, nothing is gained. I sat down at a restaurant counter and the gum-chewing waitress flipped me a menu. "What'll ya have," she asked, watching a truck driver as he pulled out of the lot.

"I'd like a piece of coconut cake and a glass of milk."

She returned in a moment with a slice of apple pie and a cup of coffee. I looked around to see if it might be someone else's order. No one was in the cafe except the cook, the waitress, and me!

I had spoken a specific, simple message directly to the waitress. She heard sounds coming from my direction and her mind ran off an old tape: "Apple pie and black coffee." She had not heard me; she was listening to the growl of that eighteen-wheeler.

A lot of communication is like that. We think if we have said it, it's been heard. We also react to things we thought were said. Effective listening concentrates on what is actually being communicated.

Some individuals don't listen because they don't know how. They've never learned to steer their mind away from themselves. Their thoughts are programmed to receive only matters that apply directly to them and their interests. They automatically reject everything else.

Some people in the church don't want to hear anything disturbing. Whenever anything controversial is brought up, they are uncomfortable. They can't bring themselves to listen to anything unpleasant.

Communicating is seldom simple. Researchers have discovered

that the general efficiency of our communication is below 50 percent. At the risk of treating the listening process as simplistic, let me suggest a few characteristics of attentive listening.

To listen *purposefully,* we must want to hear what's being said. Only when we *want* to communicate with others will we concentrate on what is being said and felt. Too much listening in church is forced, so the message doesn't get through.

In times of controversy, we seldom listen openly; we listen defensively. While the other person is talking, we mount our defense for reply. We plan what we're going to say when he stops talking. We build a wall around ourselves, so the message can't penetrate our feelings.

Sometimes we listen deceitfully. We pretend to concentrate on what is being said, while ignoring it all. *Honest* listening is trying to hear any truth being expressed, whether or not we happen to agree with the conclusion.

We assume that when we hear something, it automatically goes to our mind. The sound signals may be transmitted to the brain, but they don't necessarily engage the mind; sometimes they hook only our feelings, missing our rational senses completely. We must listen *intelligently* in order to respond reasonably. Listen to the logic of the words. Ask yourself if the reasoning is consistent. Does what is being said relate to the subject? Or is it far afield? What about the tone of the talk? Intelligence turns the lights on the conversation.

The most difficult way to listen during a dispute is *compassionately*. When we are irritated, our empathy and compassion usually retreat. Caring, compassionate listening recognizes the humanity of the speaker. Don't regard him as the devil just because he disagrees with you. Hear the pain in an angry rebuttal. Listen the way you would like to be heard. Compassion does not mean giving up your point of view, but trying to understand why the other person feels as he does. Jesus listened to many with whom he did not agree, for whom he did no miracles, but he was compassionate.

Supplication. Supplication or prayer should be a part of the total evaluating and communicating activity. At times prayer is the only thing I can do. When I don't know enough to evaluate and no one will communicate with me, prayer is always an open door to help. I pray one prayer often: "Lord, I don't know what to do, nor how to do it; show me." I start with that prayer, and God leads a step at a time. Along with that prayer, I call on a promise from God: "If any of you lacks wisdom, he should ask God, who gives generously to all without finding fault, and it will be given to him" (Jas. 1:5, NIV). In controversy, the wisdom of God is indispensable. Prayer is the avenue which will lead us to this help.

My first year in a pastorate, after seminary, I was continually harassed by a woman in our church. It wasn't anything big or threatening; she just disagreed about everything and bickered over anything. I could feel an emotional explosion building within me. While I was nearing the limit of my control, I attended a retreat at our state Baptist assembly. Dr. W. A. Criswell was the camp pastor. When he finished preaching one morning, I asked his advice in this situation. I thought he might suggest a few simple moves to help me avoid a head-on conflict with this woman.

"I don't know what to tell you to do," this experienced pastor replied. "When I get back to my church in Dallas, I've got the same problem. But I do know that you should stay on your face in prayer before God. He will guide you through."

To this day I'm grateful for that humble, simple encouragement to stay in prayer. Prayer is not all we must do, of course, but until we do pray, we cannot do anything else with assurance. We must study how to pray, then practice what we learn. If we pray as Jesus taught, we may expect God's guidance.

"And when ye stand praying, forgive . . . " (Mark 11:25). Jesus taught that our forgiving is vital to prayer. Our refusal to forgive one another is a deterrent to the Spirit of God in our churches. When we refuse to forgive, the Scriptures teach, God does not forgive us. "And whenever you stand praying, if you have anything against anyone, forgive it, so that your Father who is in heaven may forgive you your trespasses" (Mark 11:25, Barclay. See Matt. 6:14,15; 18:35; Col. 3:13). These are startling statements about the power of forgiveness. The secret resentment, the disguised anger that people harbor, is worse than we imagine. Accumulated grievances drive the Spirit of Christ from our lives. Unless we learn to forgive, our spirits will be crippled.

Jesus set a goal for us when he taught, "Be perfect, therefore, as your heavenly Father is perfect" (Matt. 5:48, NIV). The apostle John repeated that standard when he wrote, "My dear children, I write this to you so that you will not sin" (1 John 2:1, NIV). But we cannot be obedient to those teachings while harboring an unforgiving attitude in our hearts. Without practicing forgiveness, we are deceiving ourselves in our relationship to Christ.

I experienced a wounded spirit of unforgiveness after a bad church fight. The hostilities had died down, and we were tending the wounded and patching up our organizations. A lot of damage had been done by Frank, a typical young adult rebel of the sixties. If it was the establishment, Frank would challenge it. *Rewrite the laws, remove the old leaders, redistribute the power* were his bywords. Devoted to his church work, Frank was loved by many of the people. But he was fiercely independent; he suspected anyone in authority. I was never able to develop any meaningful communication with him about our differences. When it was evident that the fray was over, Frank left the church. He visited other congregations. Every time the mail came, I hoped for a request for his letter of membership; it never came.

One Sunday morning I saw Frank walk into church. My blood pressure shot up! My stomach tightened, and cold sweat gathered in the palms of my tightened fists. I had the emotional reaction of a cat seeing a dog walk into its yard.

For several Sundays he returned, sitting quietly in the services. Tension grew. Greetings between us were polite but brief and cool.

At this time I was preaching sermons on the Lord's Prayer. I had come to the phrase "Forgive us our debts,/as we also have forgiven our debtors" (Matt. 6:12, NIV). I read every sermon and commentary I could get on that verse, but no sermon came. Saturday afternoon I sat frustrated at my desk. All week long, every time I studied that verse of Scripture, Frank stood in the shadows of my mind.

Finally in desperation I turned away from my books, as though someone were standing beside my desk. I began an angry complaint to God.

I know what's the matter. You're hindering my sermon on forgiveness. I can't think, and I can't get the feeling for that verse because you are withholding your Spirit. Don't blame me. Frank's the one at fault! Look at the Scripture. It says, "How oft shall my brother sin against me, and I forgive him? till seven times?" (Matt. 18:21). *But Frank hasn't asked me even one time! Even you wait for confession before you forgive* (1 John 1:9). *Am I to be more generous than God?*

I turned back to my books. *What does forgiveness really mean?* I mused. *Does it mean, Just forget it! Act as though it didn't happen. Go ahead as though there is no difference or disagreement or wrong? Is that what forgiveness means?* I couldn't define forgiveness in a way that made sense to me.

As I studied, the meaning came: *To forgive means to remove the barriers that hinder a relationship.* If some huge obstacle stands between two people, they can't relate to each other. When that obstruction is moved aside, then they can have fellowship.

Forgiveness doesn't mean forget the barrier, or ignore the obstacle, or pay no attention to the hurt. We don't have to forget in order to forgive. It's the other way around: We must purposefully set aside the barrier to the relationship. Then when its presence does not aggravate the mind, it may gradually fade from memory.

Sometimes we practice the opposite. In order *not* to forgive, we arrange to forget. Because we will not forgive a disturbing incident, we remove ourselves purposefully from the problem. We move from the church; we leave the neighborhood; we avoid the person so we won't be reminded of a grievance. Instead of removing the obstacle from our spirit, we remove ourselves in an attempt to forget.

But in order to forgive, we must deliberately set aside the ill will and become accessible to renewing a relationship. We must not let the past offense stand in the way of reconciliation.

Another thing I learned after my complaint against God was that I had been misreading and misquoting Matthew 18:21. It does *not* read, "If my brother ask forgiveness." It doesn't mention his asking. It states, "How oft shall my brother sin against me, and I forgive him?" "Don't let anything hinder your being reconciled to your brother," Jesus was saying. "Keep the way open in your heart." Jesus didn't talk about the offender's responsibility; he talked about ours.

I pushed back my chair and turned toward God. *All right, I prayed. I understand what I'm to do. I forgive Frank.* I said this silently in my heart. Then I spoke aloud as though he were standing there: "Frank, I forgive you all the hurt and wrong I have felt." With that I turned to my typewriter and wrote my sermon for the next day.

Although I had sincerely forgiven Frank, I didn't go and tell him about it. Feeling that I should wait, I prayed about what to do.

I preached that sermon on forgiveness the next morning, hoping Frank would hear it. But he was not in church that day. One week later, on Sunday evening, as the people were gathering for worship, a terrible ice storm blew into the city. We decided to cancel the service. Everyone had left the church. I was getting ready to leave when Frank walked in. "Could I talk with you a few minutes?" he asked.

This was the first initiative Frank had taken toward me for a long time. I couldn't imagine what had happened. I had told no one of my struggle with forgiveness that Saturday afternoon.

"Brother Wallace," Frank began in his straightforward way, "you know I've been in strong disagreement with you. I've even considered joining another congregation, but I love this church. My family doesn't want to leave. I want to stay here, serve, and be happy. I want to be in a good relationship with you. I'll do what it takes to make it right."

I was stunned. I could hardly believe God had brought about a change so soon after my expression of forgiveness. It seemed as if God had been waiting on me to forgive before he got through to Frank.

When he finished, I told Frank the whole story about that Saturday afternoon and my struggle over forgiveness. Then we talked openly and honestly about our differences and how we'd like to work together in the future.

After our discussion, Frank and I knelt and prayed. In all the years since that day we have continued to work together in service to Christ as members of the fellowship of forgiveness.

7

Consequences of Conflict

The effects of conflict are infinitely varied. This makes it impossible to predict the consequences of a pending controversy. Unknown elements can bring the unexpected.

But there are general consequences which may be anticipated. From our knowledge of people and circumstances, we may foresee some likely effects. Results may be viewed from two general perspectives: the immediate and the extended outcomes of conflict. Some effects of a dispute emerge immediately. Other influences extend beyond the time of the actual struggle.

When viewing the gains and losses of a conflict, it must be emphasized that consequences are largely dependent upon how *individuals* respond to the stress. It is *the person, not the issue* which determines results. From a fight that wounds the spirit, one may emerge wiser and more compassionate; another will become a bitter cynic. Conflict, like fire, refines and destroys, softens and hardens at the same time. It is not so much what happens, although lessons may be learned from that, but it is *how a person reacts that makes the difference.* No one can determine what attitude we shall hold about an incident or a person. I am the only one responsible for how I react to insult and injury. Someone said of Hubert Humphrey: "He was immune to insult." We *can* control our immediate response to conflict.

Controversy's extended effect may evolve differently from what we expected in the heat of strife. Time and distance permit us to forgive and change. But time also allows errors to be compounded and perpetuated.

Immediate Effects. Often the first reaction to the threat of disagreement is a paralysis of the spirit. When we become aware of an adversary in our path, we pause. We stop to size up this threat to our peace and progress. We have to readjust our attitude and make some changes in our behavior.

At church we are sometimes caught unaware by a disagreement. Innocence or ignorance may lead us to an unintentional clash with fellow Christians. We are shocked when we realize that we are in an adversary position against our friends. We are stunned that those who were close to us do not think as we thought they would. What will this do to our relationship? Will we lose their friendship? Will they be as fair in controversy as they were friendly in agreement? Why don't they feel as we do? What will we do without their support? Maybe we're wrong. If we do nothing more, perhaps this problem will go away.

It may be wise to pause in our activity when a dispute emerges. We do need to adjust to new contingencies. But to remain inactive will hurt us personally and halt progress in the church. Some pastors and churches stop any action or project which arouses opposition. Soon they are confined to a small circumference of predictable activity.

I am sometimes reminded of puppet shows I've seen in churches. The use of puppets is an effective way to present gospel truths to children. Some churches have elaborate puppet ministries. But the church that is paralyzed by the fear of disagreement becomes a religious puppet show in itself. Its activities are manipulated by hidden forces of fear. Its words are only mimicked religious sounds. That church becomes a "let's pretend" place.

This paralysis of spirit keeps people from commitment to service, lest they be hurt. This fear of emotional pain paralyzes the minister and church members alike, but the pastor who does not venture beyond his anxiety lacks the very essence of leadership—personal autonomy!

I've referred to an experience when three leaders demanded that I follow their instructions in all my plans for the church. As I walked home after that confrontation, my fears screamed at me. My anxieties were both personal and professional, encompassing everything from my pride to the necessities of life. But an alarm kept ringing in the back of my mind. It warned that if I backed down in the face of these demands, I'd be running away from every showdown the rest of my life. Inactivity may have been wise in that situation if the issue had been vague. But the demand to surrender my personal autonomy was clear. I chose to act on my deepest conviction and trust the consequences to God.

The same fear and momentary paralysis came over me again in a troublesome experience twenty years later. "I hurt so badly and feel the anguish of this conflict so continually that an old wound bleeds again," I cried to my wife. "My deepest fear is not how this church struggle comes out. I'm afraid that after it's over, I'll never stand up for my convictions again." I feared a permanent paralysis of spirit.

Exposure is another immediate consequence of conflict. Our hidden qualities and flaws emerge under stress. Nothing reveals a person quite so clearly as conflict; it tears the veneer from our behavior.

In a crisis, normally unnoticed factors emerge in churches as well as individuals. We see our strengths and weaknesses when we struggle. Such knowledge is vital before we can change and grow spiritually.

Weaknesses in organizations become evident in crises. If communication has been a problem, a clamor for information will go up. If an autocratic leader has assumed too much authority, a competing power may emerge. If those who have been assigned responsibilities fail, there is a call for change. Exposure causes a shift in attitudes.

Exposure also brings a change of relationships. When the ugly side of a person has been exposed, he may not want to deal with it. Some people are unable to forgive and unwilling to confess. They do not want reconciliation—only revenge. Some withdraw from the church while others harden their spirit and await an opportunity to avenge their hurt.

But exposure elevates other Christians. There are many quiet, stalwart members in every church, unnoticed until a crisis erupts. Then they respond to need and step forward to share their strengths. I have been surprised by some unexpected help in difficult times. I have also been shocked when others have fled from the challenge.

An outgrowth of exposure is *self-knowledge*. It can be very instructive, but not every person gains new knowledge of himself from his troubles. Many people refuse to see the needs exposed by a crisis. They also fail to perceive their own motivations and reactions in a controversy.

I've learned much about myself in conflict. Although it has been painful, knowledge gained in distress has been most rewarding.

I had been in my present church for nine happy years. The church was growing, and we had made many progressive changes with very little dissension. Then a crisis arose. The need for the church to move from its location became obvious. We were the first congregation in central Kentucky to consider moving our church from an old location to a new, spacious site. We bought land, started a mission congregation on that site, and still maintained the old established church.

With all these innovations, controversy came. Relationships grew hostile. Communication bogged down. Leadership emerged as the crux of the crisis. Who will lead this church through the transition and into a new era of ministry? What style of leadership is needed in the turbulent flux of old and new ideas? How shall established relationships be preserved and the church's strength be maintained for necessary changes? How can the impossible demands be dealt with and irrational proposals be deterred? Compounding these problems was an aggressive scheme to remove me as the pastor.

My weaknesses became obvious and painful to me. Then I discovered a source of help outside my usual sphere of study. I began reading books on human relationships, personality development, and leadership styles. These were not substitutes for prayer and Bible study, but they were God's provision for a great inadequacy in my abilities.

It is strange how blind we are to our inconsistencies, especially when viewed through religious lenses. Example: I did trust God and preached the need for a life of faith. But my attitude was often negative. While calling our church members to a higher spiritual life, I sometimes preached down to them, criticizing their failures without affirming their good works. How inconsistent! I did not see that faith in God should have produced a positive, encouraging attitude.

I saw my weakness while studying leadership styles. This led me to radical personal improvements. Most of the positive developments of my own life have come in struggles of adversity. The exposure of flaws is a blessing if it's followed by change.

Any serious conflict for an extended period of time results in a *loss of momentum* in the church's ministry. The paralysis of spirit grips some people. Others are distracted from service by controversy. Goals which may have been clear become clouded. Income is affected, and future programs are threatened. "What do we do now?" becomes the insistent question.

More than once sincere friends have asked me, "If you are going to have a fight, wouldn't it be better to leave?" Members involved in strife ask themselves, "What shall we do? Fire the preacher? Leave the church? Withdraw from participation until this blows over?" Constructive momentum is lost while members redirect their energies to flee or fight.

Intense conflict distracts everyone involved and impairs their effectiveness. When people become preoccupied with the pros and cons of a dispute, they give little effort to ministry. The adage is right: "You can't fight a war and build a city at the same time."

A slowing of momentum often means a *loss of motivation*. Who has the heart to work when efforts may be shredded by criticism? "Why try?" becomes the reaction of many faced with controversy.

In severe conflict there usually is a *loss of relationships*. Few people disagree gracefully. Not many of us can oppose a friend without some loss of esteem. We keep our pride by putting the other person down; we divert attention from an issue by criticising the people involved.

While some relationships are lost because of positive disagreement, others are the result of "fallout." Victims of fallout are not directly involved in the trouble, but they just do not want to be in a climate that is not peaceful. If they sense any tension they are ill at ease, or they may have a friend who was hurt in the fray. Others feel pressured to take sides, but they can't bring themselves to do it. So they withdraw from the fellowship rather than be uncomfortable.

But of all the losses I've experienced in conflict, none have affected me so deeply as the *loss of self-esteem*. The word *esteem* means "to set a high value upon . . . to regard highly." Most people lose some self-esteem when drawn into controversy. This loss has come to me from two sources. The first is from within me. I question my own position in differing with others. *If you were competent,* I say to myself, *you'd not be in this mess! If you'd worked harder, this wouldn't have happened. If you were smart, you'd have a better solution. If you really had what it takes, you'd be at the top, like Zig! If you pleased the Lord, he said even your enemies would be at peace with you* (Prov. 16:7)*; but you have a gang of people mad at you!*

A second thing that can cause loss of self-esteem is the accusations of adversaries. Their complaints can be devastating. Those who criticize the loudest usually know the least. But realizing that doesn't stop the hurt. Every church has a gaggle of experts on "what's wrong." These Christians should have a "D.D." by their names to show that they are experts in the Discouragement and Destruction of self-esteem.

Rather than injuring another's self-esteem, the Bible tells us to "humble" ourselves (Jer. 13:18; Matt. 18:4; Jas. 4:10; 1 Pet. 5:6). It does not tell us to humble the other person; that's humiliation. Too many of us don't know the difference between humility and humiliation. One is a grace, and the other is a sin! Humility is not a denial of our good qualities. Humility attributes to God all the good one has and accepts responsibility for his own failures. But humiliation condemns the good along with the bad. Humility recognizes its own excellence without being proud. But humiliation takes pride in magnifying another's weakness.

When our failures are exploited, we lose self-esteem. We feel that if we'd done differently, we would not be in a controversy. Sometimes this is true, but self-flagellation never solved a problem.

In periods of severe conflict, I've suffered the loss of self-esteem until I dropped into a pit of deep depression. Despair engulfed me and self-hate raged. Had I not received the strong support of my wife and encouragement from a few friends, I might not have survived professionally. The loss of self-esteem must be stopped, or it will bleed the spirit to death.

During these experiences I have discovered ways of restoring self-esteem. First, I listen to friends and believe some of the affirming things they say. I know them to be honest. I accept the positive qualities they say I have.

Next, I look at myself and acknowledge what I *know* to be good about myself. No matter what others say, I know where I am capable and sincere. I name my good characteristics aloud, as though I am talking to someone who needs my honest encouragement. I know the truth, accept it, and lift my head.

When I listen to others and can affirm myself, I am able to hear the voice of God again. His promises infuse me with new courage. I don't cease to read the Word of God and plead in prayer, but in my depression these usually become a rote exercise.

There is another discipline I use to rebuild my self-esteem. Because self-worth is built on the experience of success, I search for areas where I have succeeded. They are there but usually hidden by self-doubt. I set short-term goals, reach them quickly, and bask in the feeling of success in little things. I also gain a feeling of worth by accomplishing small but significant attainments in areas outside my church. Some of them are physical activities; others are hobbies I do well. I concentrate on my accomplishments, commit past failures to God, and go ahead planning to win.

Along with these moves I have learned to quit comparing myself with anyone else. I still wrestle with that devil Envy, but I win more often now. I'm learning that happiness comes easier when I accept my own uniqueness in the providence of God.

I have also found affirmation from groups outside my church. I've taken courses at the University of Kentucky where I received feedback and counsel on my conflict behavior. Selected continuing education at Southern Baptist Seminary has been vital to my renewals. Seminars provided by the Sunday School Board have given me needed direction when I was bogged down mentally. Reactions from my peers in pastor-support groups have been invaluable. All these people had nothing at stake in my conflicts, so they observed and commented objectively. This positive climate has made it possible for me to test my attitudes against their judgment. From this has emerged affirmation and guidance for renewed activity.

In church conflicts there are other immediate losses, such as money and membership. These are not to be taken lightly, but I feel they are given too much concern. When individuals aspire to find and do the will of God, tangible losses like these are compensated by other rewards.

The Extended Effects of Conflict. With every controversy there are extended effects as well as immediate consequences. Sometimes we ignore the need to deal with future results. We say, "Time will heal everything." What we mean is, "We'll forget, and things will return as they were."

Time passes, but it does not heal. The days and years allow us opportunity to bring about healing. Time is merely a frame in which we grow or atrophy. What we do determines the extended consequences of a conflict.

The immediate outcome of a dispute is certainly significant. However, results which stretch into the future are equally important. Ultimate effects are often different from what we anticipated in the throes of dispute. Time permits developments which cannot be realized in the fray of confrontation.

In the providence of God I have served one congregation thirty-three years. In this time the church has accomplished many things. We have also had conflicts of varying dimensions. The people and I have learned and changed together. This much time gives a unique vantage point for viewing extended effects of controversies. Now I see three major areas of growth which have come from conflicts. These developments are in the areas of *personality, perspective,* and *power.*

In these spheres are possibilities of negative consequences. But for this discussion I will emphasize some positive benefits.

From the most painful clashes there can emerge tremendous growth in our personalities. We also can develop keen perception and wider perspective in human relationships. And in the frightening struggles with adversaries, new power can be generated within us.

Personality. The Bible gives numerous illustrations of dramatic personality changes brought about through conflict. Jacob, Moses, Joseph, Daniel, Peter, and Paul are familiar examples of those who were changed through severe struggle.

Perfection for daily living is not given us suddenly. We are "babes in Christ" (1 Cor. 3:1) before we grow up into Christ in all things

(Eph. 4:14-15). Such growth can come out of conflict. One of the effects which I value from my own struggles has been the change within myself. Foremost in this personality change is the development of flexibility in my attitude and manner. In youth my religious environment was that of extreme dogmatism. There was only one point of view in every situation. Rigidity and ridicule were the defense against any difference of opinion. Disagreements were always a challenge to controversy. Flexibility was not in the vocabulary of my mentors.

Many Christians today fear this word *flexible*. They equate it with a lack of convictions. They interpret it as synonymous with weakness. But to be flexible does not mean to be flaccid. A flaccid muscle in the body has lost shape and strength. It lacks resilience and energy. The same applies to a flaccid personality. It lacks strength to resist and power to act. When forced to decide, the flaccid person always moves in the channel of least resistance. To be flaccid is vastly different from being flexible.

Akin to the flaccid person is the rigid individual. His expressions are always in the absolute. His convictions are dogmatic and his views myopic. In conflict I discovered two characteristics of a rigid person. I found these within myself and by observing other people embroiled in controversy. The rigid person is either insecure or insensitive—often both.

The rigid individual is usually insecure about the beliefs he holds. He may defend them vociferously, but he is not sure of them. He is afraid to venture from the comfortable position he holds about a matter, lest he cannot return. He is apprehensive of change and intimidated by questions. The inflexible defender refuses to admit his attitude. "No, I'm not upset." "No, nothing's bothering me." "Everything's all right." "It doesn't matter." These are verbally closed doors to feelings the speaker would hide. He does not want to change his attitudes; therefore, he will not subject them to discussion. The rigid man is restrained by fear; he lacks courage to explore new solutions to problems. That's why insecurity prompts us to "hold what we've got" and not flex enough to consider another attitude.

The rigid person is often insensitive to other points of view. He may be touchy as a sunburn about his own feelings, yet completely indifferent to how anyone else feels. He is absorbed in *his* view, and nothing else. Insensitivity doesn't make the effort to understand why another is in disagreement.

When I was trying to get a home of my own I was stunned by the insensitivity of many people. They had the security of home ownership. They enjoyed the advantages of having their own houses. Yet, of all the people that opposed us owning our home, only two families inquired as to why we felt as we did. I was invited to one home to discuss my reasons. "Pastor, we don't agree with you, but we'd like you to tell us why you don't want to live in a parsonage." When I finished explaining how our family felt about it they replied, "We'd never thought of those things. Now we understand why you feel this way."

Rigidity hardens opposition. Rigidity blinds us to reconciliation. The rigid person does not consider alternatives. He will not take time and effort to explore all reasonable approaches to a problem.

When wagons were the mode of transportation, the wheels were made of wood, covered with a steel rim. Such a wheel had no flexibility. It did not yield to any obstacle in its path. So the steel rim wore out quickly and had to be replaced often. Later a solid rim of rubber covered the wheels. These flexed some and absorbed small shocks. Today the modern tire gives a better ride and lasts many times longer than those old wagon wheels.

In time I learned to be more flexible. The alternatives were that I'd be broken or wear out soon. Flexibility, like the modern automobile tire, does have its limits, yet yields enough to absorb the harsh impact of opposing forces.

There are several elements in a flexible personality; *patience* is one of them. It is sometimes necessary to wait for developments that time alone can bring. Paul wrote, "Tribulation worketh patience" (Rom. 5:3). Conflict is the arena where patience is learned. A wise man helped impress upon me the value of patience one day with this gentle rebuke: "Pastor, sometimes a handful of patience is worth a bucket full of brains."

Patience doesn't always mean stopping what you are doing. It more often means shifting into low gear and easing through rough places. Patience is the high-wire walker at the circus. Patience doesn't have to race to the goal. Of course, there are time limits in living; but in most cases of disagreement, we will save time by being patient. When I've acted impulsively and forced premature action, the backlash has come. Then I've spent more time restoring relationships than I would have spent being patient in the beginning.

Flexibility involves another skill: *tact!* Someone has said that tact is the ability to charm a porcupine into a possum. Too many times I've kicked the porcupine! Sometimes I've kicked a possum and been shocked when he turned into a porcupine.

Tact is the grace Paul taught us when he wrote: "And be ye kind one to another" (Eph. 4:32). If you lack tact, try being kind to your adversary.

I shall never forget an afternoon's visit to the home of a woman who had stopped coming to church. I learned that she was upset by words I had said involving a friend of hers. I admitted, "Yes, I said those things in a sermon, but I spoke the truth."

"You spoke the truth all right, but you were not kind."

The flexible person is sensitive to mood and feeling. He tries to learn what others feel in a confrontation. A flexible leader tries to find the motivation behind hostility. He is sensitive to feelings as well as facts, to emotion as well as reason.

Being sensitive does not mean being afraid of emotion. We need to be sensitive to another's aggravation without being threatened by it. When we find out why he is angry, we will have a point from which to begin reconciliation. The flexible person says, "I want to know how you *feel* about this."

One of the most difficult things I've had to learn is that feelings are as important as facts in relationship—sometimes more so. I've had all the facts on my side, but people were against me because I was not sensitive to feelings. Only when I flexed enough to understand their feelings was I able to get communication flowing again. When I accepted their strong feelings, then they gave me the right to share my point of view.

Flexibility is the capacity to change directions without losing sight of the goal. It is the skill to set the sail differently in an adverse wind and still move to your original destination.

Even the naturally flexible person has rough spots in his personality which conflict can refine. But such changes take time and reflection to develop. Although it is not the most desirable way to change, strife can improve our personality in ways we did not anticipate.

Perspective. Another benefit I have drawn from experiences in controversy has been the development of a broader perspective for my faith. For me the most valuable aspect of this enlarged perspective was to learn that God has resources beyond our imagination.

Paul affirmed that God "is able to do exceeding abundantly above all that we ask or think. . . . " (Eph. 3:20). I had preached enthusiastically on God's miracles of provision; but only when I experienced being without any solutions to problems in conflict did I get new insight of God's power to provide.

Our small-town church had a pretty building, but the lighting in the sanctuary was poor. Three antiquated light fixtures hung from a high ceiling. One day I mentioned to the leading man in the church (who was also the treasurer) that new light fixtures might improve the church. His only reply was a grunt I couldn't interpret. I suggested the idea to others. Vague replies were the only response. No one told me that the treasurer himself had hung those fixtures long ago.

Later I baptized a young businessman into our fellowship. He was eager to do what he could for his church. One Sunday night he observed, "These are the poorest lights I ever saw. Makes me feel like I'm attending a séance rather than a church service. Why don't we get some new lights?"

I was elated. I went back to the treasurer and asked about the possibility of hanging some new fixtures. This time he replied, "We don't have the money, and we don't believe in special collections."

When I explained this to the young businessman, he volunteered, "I'll buy the lights and pay for hanging them. I'm way behind on what I owe the Lord."

There was only one electrician in town. We engaged him to hang the lights. A few days after Ellis had promised to install the lights he came by the parsonage and said, "Preacher, I can't hang those lights for you. The wiring's not safe. The building would catch on fire."

"Then let's make the building safe. I'm sure the people would want to remove any hazard to a fire."

"No, preacher, I'm not going to hang those lights, no matter what. Clint says he doesn't want them hung, and you know I do a lot of work for Clint. I can't hang them."

The lights were already in transit. When they arrived, Ellis phoned from his shop. "I'm going to ship them back tomorrow because there ain't anybody around here that'll hang 'em."

I wondered, *How am I going to explain this kind of impasse to a new Christian? What effect will it have on his attitude toward the church? Lord, I don't know what to do or say.*

I was walking down Main Street, which was also the highway through town. There was very little traffic, but as I neared my friend's store I saw a pickup truck driving slowly toward me. On the door was "M & M Electricians, Boulder, Colo." They were several hundred miles from home. I strode into the street and hailed them. "Hey, what are you fellows doing so far from home?"

The truck stopped. Its occupants said, "We're driving south looking for work. Do you know where we can get a job?"

"If you're honest-to-goodness electricians you can go to work right now!"

They hung the lights, rewired the building, and settled in that town to start a thriving business.

God doesn't always provide in ways so timely and dramatic. But in many unforeseen ways he has met my needs and so enlarged faith's perspective. In addition, conflict has been the arena where I've learned the effective use of power.

Power. In churches the word *power* is anathema except when associated in a nebulous manner with some spiritual exercise. In the church power becomes suspect when it is applied to personal relationships. If we can adorn power with some spiritual mandate, then we can talk about it acceptably.

This confined view of power inhibits our understanding of its use. Power is neither good nor bad; it is neutral. Power is simply the ability to get results. With power, influence is exercised over people, situations, and oneself. If you want to get anything done, you must use power. It has been over an extended period that I've gradually learned some things about the use of power. There are three things that we do with power. We use power, we abuse power, and we lose power. This is especially so when we are embroiled in conflict. It took quite a bit of time and some experience in conflict to learn that power is to be used. Our abilities, capacities, and influence are inseparable from life. If we don't use them, we are guilty of the same sin as the man who buried his talent in the ground. It was given to him for use. But he wouldn't take the risk that came with exercising his power of investment. When we have disagreements we often refuse to use our power. When influence is needed during controversy, we sometimes feel that it would be wrong to use our skills in resolving the crisis, but there *is* an authentic use of power in conflict. We need to be sure we are using it authentically, not abusively.

Four distinct elements characterize the authentic use of power. If these are lacking, we abuse power.

Credentials. The first element needed to develop authentic character in the exercise of power is to have credentials rooted in assigned authority. Too many people get into a controversy that is not their responsibility. If a committee is assigned a problem to solve, they, not others, are responsible for working out the solution. Credentials consist of assigned responsibility and authority to get a job done.

Competence lends authenticity to power. If trouble is to be resolved, people who are competent must deal with the particular problem. Lack of knowledge and skill leads to failure. For example: A person with no experience in music could likely not help resolve differences about the church music program. Personnel problems need aid from those with human relation skills. Scripture stresses the use of power in areas of our competence when it teaches that the Holy Spirit gives different gifts to people (1 Cor. 12).

David showed wisdom when he refused Saul's armor. It didn't fit, and he wasn't trained to handle it. Later David wore his own armor, but he always moved within his own competence. Some people try to use their power with Saul's armor. It adorns their ego, but it doesn't win the battle.

Courage. Some Christians have abilities they are afraid to use. They are qualified, but they lack the courage to exercise power. Courage is an indispensable element of authentic power. Some lack courage because they fear failure; others may not wish to offend. They hold authority apologetically and use power timidly. Courage clothes power with authenticity.

We misunderstand the character of courage if we think it is a lack of fear. Courage is not the absence of fear; it is the mastery of fear.

The supreme illustration of that truth occurred when Jesus arose from Gethsemane and called to the disciples, "Up! Let's go! The traitor is coming!" Then he walked with dignity to meet Judas.

In all kinds of conflict—individual disagreements or struggles involving many people—courage needs to have more qualities than simple boldness. For one thing, courage has the image of *confrontation.* When a person makes vague insinuations, many people in the church are reluctant to confront him and demand clarity and truth.

"They said the children's department is not teaching the Bible to the children."

"Who is 'they' and what are they teaching?" This is a needed question of confrontation to help solve problems and stop dissension. Generalities and ambiguities are the termites of fellowship. Every situation does not call for confrontation; but when one does, courage must move with power to contest wrong.

Along with boldness to confront there must also be *confession.* The intensity of confrontation sometimes breaks down restraint and ignores gracious speech. In controversy all of us make mistakes. But the fact that we are imperfect is no excuse for us to ignore our errors.

The person brave enough to deal with his own faults will grow in power to influence others. Nothing placates an adversary like sincere apology. Nothing curtails criticism like confession. When we err, the sooner we say, "I was wrong; I'm sorry," the more effective it will be to heal relationships.

Courage needs the aggressive elements of confrontation and confession. But courage will wane if it lacks the quality of *continuance.* It takes tremendous courage to keep on doing the right thing, whether there are signs of progress or not. There have been times when I would rather have taken a beating than to have met with a committee or to have gone to a congregational business meeting! But to go and face the unpleasant confrontation was the right thing to do.

In a support group a pastor was discussing a problem. "I have a person in my church always on my back. He's always criticizing, always complaining, always challenging me—no matter what I do." He turned to me: "John, do you ever have that?"

"Sometimes."

"What do you do?"

"It depends upon the particular circumstances. Occasionally, I have to take the attitude David took toward Shimei when Shimei followed him cursing and throwing stones. David said, 'Let him alone, and let him curse . . . It may be that the Lord will look on mine affliction, and that the Lord will requite me good for his cursing this day' (2 Sam. 16:5-13). Sometimes it's best to silently endure while you continue your course."

David could have exercised his kingly privilege and let Abishai cut off Shimei's head. But David simply continued down the road, enduring Shimei.

It is interesting what happened to Shimei. He outlived David and prospered. God doesn't always set everything right the next day. Years later King Solomon called Shimei before him: "Thou knowest all the wickedness which thine heart is privy to, that thou didst to David my father: therefore the Lord shall return thy wickedness upon thine own head" (1 Kings 2:44).

"Do not be deceived: God cannot be mocked. A man reaps what he sows" (Gal. 6:7, NIV).

Finally, I mention an activity not often associated with courage, but I believe it's necessary in resolving many conflicts. It is the ability to *compromise*. *Compromise* is usually a bad word to Christians. But in most disagreements, there are things we can give up without surrendering basic values. Many times we can concede vocabulary, procedures, pride, and some advantages we hold in argument. Our problem here is that we fear people may perceive compromise as weakness. To the contrary, only the courageous can offer to compromise without feeling threatened.

Control is also an essential element to courage. Daring sometimes replaces discipline in battle. But courage must be under control. The preacher wrote in Proverbs, "A fool gives full vent to his anger, but a wise man keeps himself under control" (29:11, NIV). Self-control is the restraining force that gives dignity to power in human relationships.

These are some of the possible effects of conflict which may develop after strife has ceased. With time, personality can be improved. Reflections over the years bring a perspective that strengthens faith. And the proper concept of power emerges with use and refinement.

8

Controlling Conflict

Control is a powerful word that radiates authority, elicits admiration, and inflames envy. Control is an imperative word that commands response and governs actions. Control is also a word of beauty, admired in an athlete's skill, and detected in the cadence of an orator. But control can be a frightening word if it symbolizes repression and privation.

What is control? Control is power to influence. It is the authority to decree what shall and shall not be.

Control is the skill to move people and events toward desired goals. It is the energy to motivate dreams into activity—a magnet that attracts what it desires.

Control is understanding and comprehension; it is discernment of the real need at a given moment.

Control is the regulation of behavior and restraint of undesirable forces. It's the pressure that overcomes adversity.

Control is a system that leads from a clear purpose to a logical and predictable sequence.

Control is the vitality to transform and the persuasion to change attitudes. Control is the key to creativity and success.

Without control chaos and failure are sure to come. Uncontrolled energies are dissipated and goals are never reached. Hope dies, and efforts are wasted when restraints are lost. Controls are essential to order and progress.

But in the context of human relations we resent the idea of control. We feel that it infringes upon our freedom and human individuality. Especially in the church we abhor the suggestion that someone needs to be in control. Christianity is life lived under the dominion of *God*. We sometimes want to believe that his authority moves in spheres unrelated to our behavior among people.

Because imperfect human nature sometimes overwhelms our spiritual nature, we must exercise control. Paul admonished, "Everything should be done in a fitting and orderly way" (1 Cor. 14:40, NIV). If control is needed in the normal functioning of life, it is even more necessary in times of controversy.

Most conflict begins as a clash with some rule or restraint. But how shall control be established and to whom shall it first be applied? Shall we impose numerous restraints upon the minister of a church? Would it be wise to define guidelines for the deacons? Shall we have rigid rules to govern the congregation? In a church where relationship is voluntary, how can control be legislated? In a faith that declares the freedom of each believer's priesthood, can boundaries be drawn?

Control is necessary in all relationships. But where should it begin? Discussing controls among Christians is like talking about taxes to citizens; everyone thinks they should begin with the other person!

I've learned most of my lessons in control the hard way. I remember one occasion when our church was in a terrible dispute over church bylaws. We were fighting for places of authority and reins of power. This conflict started when one committee's action displeased those outside the power structure. Then came the controversy over who would have control. The contention evolved to the point where the whole church was in confusion.

I went to a wise counselor who was not a member of my church. After describing the situation, I concluded in despair, "I don't know what to do to bring the church under control."

"John, you can't govern anyone but yourself! You are the only one over whom you have complete control."

"Right now," I replied, "I've nearly lost touch with myself."

"You have to master your emotions and thought processes. When you can govern yourself, your example will influence others."

So I began to take the steps necessary to get hold of my feelings and thoughts. Through that crisis and many others along the way, I've learned to regulate myself first. I have discovered four areas where control must be developed. Control must begin within the spirit of a person. Then it can be directed by study, strengthened by structure, and exercised by strategy.

Spirit. Control always begins *within* a person. We must control our own attitudes and feelings before we can hope to govern forces beyond ourselves. The writer of Proverbs emphasized the spirit's control: "He who is slow to anger is better than the mighty,/And he who rules his spirit,/than he who captures a city" (16:32, NASV).

A person in control of himself radiates power. Especially during conflict, a person with self-control possesses a unique dynamic within a group. If he has a rein on his feelings and knows what he believes, he can influence others.

When I use the word *spirit,* I mean attitudes and feelings, beliefs and thought processes. The spirit is that force of mind and will which activates physical and emotional energies.

Control of the spirit starts with *belief.* Thomas J. Watson, Jr., builder of IBM, lays the foundation for success when he states:

> I firmly believe that any organization, in order to survive and achieve success, must have a sound set of beliefs on which it premises all its policies and actions.
>
> Next I believe that the most important single factor in corporate success is faithful adherence to those beliefs. And finally, I believe that if an organization is to meet the challenges of a changing world, it must be prepared to change everything about itself except those beliefs as it moves through corporate life.[1]

If this is true for a materialistic effort, it is even more essential for the church. Clear beliefs are imperatives for the Christian who wants to get control of himself and exert constructive influence. We must first develop a believing spirit. With what beliefs do we face the crises of life?

When Jesus prepared his disciples for their most traumatic trials, he began by saying, "Believe in God, believe also in me. . . . believe me for the very works' sake" (John 14:1-11). Our Lord drove down great stakes of belief against fear and despair. He knew that what the disciples believed would determine how they would respond to crises. So with us; what we believe determines what we do. If we do not know what to believe, or do not believe strongly, we will be like leaves in the wind. When in some storm of controversy I clarify firmly what I believe, control begins to form, almost like something physical.

To develop control of self, you must also want self-control intensely! When Jesus faced people with problems, he sometimes asked, in effect, "What do you want?" (Matt. 20:32; John 5:6). Often in conflict we are not sure what we want or to what degree we desire it.

"I would do anything to avoid controversy!" a pastor remarked to me. He knew he wanted to avoid a fight. And he did!

In the midst of a lengthy controversy I found myself obsessed with the conviction that a certain member should leave the church. To me, he was a key troublemaker. I became aware that first on my list of desires was the removal of this member.

Things got so bad I finally prayed about it. That may sound fatuous, but it's not! We usually don't seek God's will very seriously when we are in controversy. We're too occupied with immediate circumstances to reach out for the ultimate purpose of God in the matter. We may *say prayers* when we're angry, but we seldom really *pray*. There is a difference in the two.

Finally I decided I wanted deliverance from my contention more than I wanted to be rid of that person, so I prayed:

"Lord, deliver our church from the evil of this continuous bickering.

"Deliver by redemption. If someone involved needs the transformation of genuine salvation, bring that about.

"Or deliver by raising us above the influence of this person's threats.

"Or deliver by removal from this church—him or me—whichever you want.

"Or deliver by restraint; protect the church against hurtful influences.

"Or deliver by revival. Bring a spiritual renewal in me and in him so that we are all controlled by thy Holy Spirit."

I wrote that prayer in my notebook and prayed it until the answer came. Emotional relief and personal control began when I decided I wanted what God wanted. Writing it down and staying with it was part of my expression of genuine desire.

For me the third factor that aids control of my spirit is the attitude of *openness*. We may have strong beliefs; we can know precisely what we want; but if we are not open and honest the spirit will become rigid and blind.

There is a psychological test for measuring openness of personality. It is called the "Johari Window." I've taken it several times over the years. By a series of questions it measures a person's willingness to expose or share his feelings with others and a person's inclination to receive feedback or information from others.

The purpose of the "Johari Window" is to show a person's strengths and weaknesses in interpersonal relationships. The test has many surprising applications. It shows that when a person shares his own feelings and receives information readily from others, he automatically knows more about himself! He becomes more skilled in his relationships with others when he gives and receives information easily. The test also demonstrates that it is necessary to share oneself in order to develop a greater understanding of other people.

A parallel to this truth of human nature is found in two verses about Jesus. Peter wrote of Jesus, "Neither was guile found in his mouth" (1 Pet. 2:22). Jesus was not a closed, deceptive person. He was open and genuine about himself. He answered questions about himself, and he also listened intently to others. "He knew all men, And needed not that any should testify of man," John wrote about Jesus, "for he knew what was in man" (John 2:24,25). The sharing and seeking spirit develops profound understanding of human nature. And understanding brings control.

Study. Although control begins with a right spirit, it cannot be sustained by attitude alone. If we do not fortify our spirit with pertinent knowledge, we will lose control to emotional forces. If knowledge is power, then study is control's link to that dynamic.

Study of control must begin with an understanding of our own strengths and weaknesses. Some people never develop control of themselves because they will not examine their lives. They dismiss any reference to a need to change by replying, "That's just the way I am." They turn off the light and close the door to self-study. They dismiss any consideration of self-improvement.

Study by reflection can make us aware of weaknesses in our

control over self. Such contemplation can bring unexpected benefit if we'll make the needed changes. If we excuse our faults or ignore our weaknesses, these flaws will cripple control when we are pressured.

We should examine our behavior in various situations, especially under stress. We should admit our mistakes and affirm what we do right. This will increase our skills and strengthen control in difficult circumstances.

Study through reading is another good opportunity for learning. Control can be learned and refined by reading. In recent years books about conflict management, leadership skills, and human relations have been written from the Christian perspective. Too long we have ignored the need for Christians to learn to deal with conflict in constructive ways. We have hurt one another shamefully in the way we've disagreed. We've taught love but ignored practical ways to implement Christian grace into our experiences of controversy.

Conflict drives me to study. I read routinely for my preaching and counseling. But during conflicts I have periods of intense study in areas which affect behavior in that crisis.

Conflict study began for me more than twenty years ago when I was faced with problems in human relationships. I regret that I was not taught conflict management when I was in seminary. Very little of that kind of information is given to students. Dedicated men and women go to serve Christ with little information on the arts of self-control and human relationships. When inevitable confrontations come, they are unprepared to follow their Lord's admonition to be "wise as serpents, and harmless as doves" (Matt. 10:16). This kind of behavior doesn't come naturally! It is the result of intense discipline.

Because this book does not include a bibliography, a limited list of helpful books is imperative. The following resources have helped me. Some emphasize the Christian perspective; others do not.

Personal Development. Books in this category teach control in conflict through good self-image and a positive mental attitude toward life. Most of us have been influenced with strong negative attitudes in home and church. Thus our reactions are often critical of others, discounting self and doubting God. The following books have helped me change my negative attitudes and poor self-image. This change has improved my skills in relating to people.

Battista, Orlando A., *The Power to Influence People.* Englewood Cliffs, N.J.: Prentice-Hall, Inc., 1959. The author was an executive of a large chemical company. This has been the most helpful book I have ever read in helping me relate to people—perhaps because I first read it at a time of great personal crisis.

Gardner, John W., *Self-Renewal.* New York: Harper & Row, 1963. An articulate scholar, Gardner stresses the necessity of self-renewal. This is not a book on religious renewal but innovation and change in the personal life.

Garn, Roy, *The Magic Power of Emotional Appeal.* Englewood Cliffs, N.J.: Prentice-Hall, Inc., 1960. Garn writes convincingly of the force of emotions in human relations. He is a realist in the fine points of personal relationship. We are usually unaware of the emotional power of our words and manners. Emotional reactions are inevitable in all relationships. Emotions, more than facts, often make the difference in control.

Giblin, Les, *How to Have Confidence and Power in Dealing with People.* Englewood Cliffs, N.J.: Prentice-Hall, Inc., 1979. This book has gone through thirty-six printings! It is a basic book on human relations. Giblin is an acknowledged leader in this field.

Hodnett, Edward, *The Art of Working with People.* New York: Harper & Row, 1959. Hodnet divided his excellent book into sections on Understanding Problems, People, Communication, and Negotiation. The section on communication was the most helpful to me. In that division these sentences caught me.

"The first step in communicating with other people is to convey correctly your attitude at a given time. Much of your effort must therefore go toward building up *acceptance of attitude,* rather than merely acceptance of your position" (p. 84).

Maltz, Maxwell, *Psycho-Cybernetics.* New York: Simon and Schuster, 1960. Dr. Maltz, a famous plastic surgeon, gained new fame by writing this best-seller on self-image. He wrote in the preface, "The 'self image' is the key to human personality and human behavior. . . . The 'self image' sets the boundaries of individual accomplishment. . . . Expand the self image and you expand the 'area of the possible'" (p. ix). This is a profound and practical book on personal development.

Leadership. It is important for anyone in a leadership position to study books on this subject. A person may be a natural leader, but he will not go far without more knowledge and skill than nature gave him. Much of this knowledge can be gained from reading.

Dayton, Edward R., and Ted W. Engstrom, *Strategy for Leadership*. Old Tappan, New Jersey: Fleming H. Revell Co., 1979. This book is about leadership in the Christian organization. Its purpose is stated in the Introduction: "The strategy for Christian leadership, then, is to help the organization . . . sort out its priorities, and build God-honoring plans to move the organization forward. That is what this book is all about." It also includes a helpful bibliography and index.

Engstrom, Ted W., *The Making of a Christian Leader*. Grand Rapids, Michigan: Zondervan Publishing House, 1976. Here is a thorough, sensitive treatment on personal leadership. Engstrom's thesis is that personal qualities in Christian leaders must be linked with an understanding of management and human relation skills. The author begins with a biblical basis for leadership from the Old and New Testaments. The book has an index of subjects and Scripture references.

Gangel, Kenneth O., *Competent to Lead*. Chicago: Moody Press, 1976. The author is an experienced administrator in Christian institutions. In the Introduction of this very practical book he writes: "Many of God's people have not yet learned how to get along with each other in a fellowship of mutual service for Christ. Short tenures of pastors, directors of Christian education, and youth ministers testify to their inability to win the battles of human relations, both among themselves and in the wider congregational context." Gangle writes for the members in a church as well as the professional leaders. Footnotes and a varied bibliography will guide the reader to further study.

Zaleznik, Abraham, *Human Dilemmas of Leadership*. New York: Harper & Row, 1966. Here is a profound study of a leader's relationship to his organization. It deals with personality conflicts on different levels. Zaleznik is professor of organizational behavior at Harvard University's Graduate School of Business Administration. He is also an affiliate member and research fellow of the Boston Psychoanalytic Society. This scholarly book is written within the disciplines of secular classroom study and industrial management.

The author's insights into human behavior are easily transferable to situations in Christian organizations. The book carries a thorough index.

Conflict Management. Books in this field from the Christian perspective are few. But industry, business, and politics have grappled with this subject for a long time. It is time that Christians began a serious study of how to manage their disagreements. Following are a few of the books I've found practical.

Boulding, Kenneth E., *Conflict and Defense: A General Theory.* New York: Harper & Row, 1968. This is a classic on the subject. It is *must* reading for every student of conflict management.

Cohen, Herb, *You Can Negotiate Anything.* Secaucus, N.J.: Lyle Stuart Inc., 1980. Cohen is a professional negotiator of international reputation. His chapter on power is worth the price of the book. "Power is based upon perception," he says. "If you think you've got it, then you've got it. If you think you don't have it, even if you've got it, then you don't have it." Cohen's humor vividly illustrates his practical instruction.

Harris, John C., *Stress, Power and Ministry.* Washington, D.C.: The Alban Institute, Inc., 1977. This book deserves wide reading by ministers and those who work with them. Harris is an Episcopal minister, but he speaks with sensitive insight to every pastor. The author's verbose style and scholarly vocabulary may discourage the casual reader. But for the serious student, it's worth the digging. The book also addresses congregational problems in matters of power, roles, and relationships.

Leas, Speed, and Paul Kittlaus, *Church Fights: Managing Conflict in the Local Church.* Philadelphia: The Westminister Press, 1973. These men did pioneer writing about conflict management in the church. The book deserves a listing in every bibliography on conflict management for Christians.

McSwain, Larry L., and William C. Treadwell, Jr., *Conflict Ministry in the Church.* Nashville: Broadman Press, 1981. This is the first book on conflict management for the local church from the perspective of Southern Baptists. Both authors have had experience in the local church and as seminary professors. McSwain and Treadwell bring compassion with their experience to this subject. The book has both theory and practical illustrations. It deserves to be in every church library, although its scholarly style may limit reading by laymen. Helpful footnotes and a full bibliography add value to the book.

Smith, Donald P., *Clergy in the Cross Fire: Coping with Role Conflicts in the Ministry*. Philadelphia: The Westminister Press, 1973. This book deals with the role conflicts of a pastor. He is in the "cross fire" of many expectations by his congregation. This necessarily involves confusion over the church's nature and mission. From such ambiguity comes conflict. This book is especially valuable to young men just beginning their ministry, since the early years involve more stress in defining roles and setting priorities.

There are two other reading sources in the area of conflict management. The Fuller Theological Seminar offers a course on "Conflict Management in the Local Church." With the course's materials comes a mimeographed bibliography. It is a thorough reading list, divided into eight categories.

The Church Administration Department of the Sunday School Board of the Southern Baptist Convention, Nashville, Tennessee, has issued a limited bibliography on conflict. It has a score of titles.

Besides these avenues of personal reflection and reading, there is one other approach to study—personal counsel. This third source of learning offers a unique dimension to exercising control.

If you want to live smart, there is no substitute for interaction with other points of view than your own. This the Bible affirms: "Listen to advice and accept instruction,/and in the end you will be wise" (Prov. 19:20, NIV).

But one of the last things most of us do in trouble is to seek counsel. We tend to worry about the quandary we are in until our mind is a whirlpool. We may even read books that improve our perspective, but we're reluctant to talk with anyone about the conflict. The Bible urges us to seek counsel, especially when we are in a controversy. "Make plans by seeking advice;/if you wage war, obtain guidance" (Prov. 20:18, NIV).

Why is it that we are so slow to seek counsel when we are having problems? Pride hinders our going to someone for suggestions on improving our relationship with other people. We all admit we're not perfect. But pride persuades us to act as though we were. By pride I'm not referring to reasonable self-esteem. Pride is that inordinate conceit that sets a person above his associates. But when pride lifts us up, it also isolates us from those we need.

In the beginning stages of conflict, we should go for help immediately. The fire department tells us to call them when even a little fire breaks out. They know that a small fire can get out of control, especially when fought alone by an inexperienced person.

Fear is a companion of pride. Pride often turns to Fear for advice, and they both agree to "go it alone." We are afraid of what someone will think if they learn we are losing control. We are afraid some will refuse their help. There's also a fear that we'll not agree with their advice.

The big fear for me is that I'll show my ignorance! None of us want to appear out of touch and unaware; we want to seem all-knowing and all-wise! In a crisis we are afraid to expose the weaknesses of our inadequacies. But the best way to overcome fear is to face it, grasp it, drag it into the light, and deal with it. The best light upon our fears often comes from the counsel of competent friends.

For many years I have been a member of a support group of pastors. We share our problems and joys. We laugh and weep together. We reveal our fears and share our opinions. One morning a young pastor came to the group, obviously upset. He told us that the day before, a deacon had rung his doorbell with the blunt announcement that he planned to declare the pulpit vacant at the next business meeting on Wednesday night.

The pastor had been in the church long enough to know that some people were never happy with any pastor. But this came as a shock. He did not know the cause of this threat or how to prepare for the confrontation.

The support group suggested ways he might handle the matter when it came to the floor. The deacon did stand and make the motion in a business meeting. But the pastor had himself well under control. He conducted the proceeding so skillfully that the move to fire him was averted. After that he continued to serve the church even more effectively than before.

If that pastor had not risked showing his fears to the support group, he could have lost control of himself even before the meeting.

That was possibly the intent of the abrupt warning by the deacon. If the pastor was thrown into panic, he might make bungling mistakes which could be used against him.

I've discovered deep within myself a hidden cause for my reluctance to seek counsel. It is envy. *I know as much as he does,* I tell myself. *He's just lucky to be so successful. He's not as spiritually minded as I. If he had my problems, he'd not handle them as well as I do.* Envy is a blinding, isolating plague. It keeps us from going to some very capable people who might give us valuable counsel. Some of the most helpful advice I've received has been from people whom I once envied. Because I envied them, I avoided them. But when I ventured to talk with them about some problems, I gained new perspectives and fresh encouragement.

If pride, fear, and envy keep you from counsel, you are already losing control! Regain control through counsel. Go to a person who could help. Say to him:

"I have a problem I'd like to tell you about."

"What is your opinion on what I've said?"

"What would you suggest?"

If you receive advice with which you do not agree, don't debate it. If you want to test his opinions in order to strengthen your own perspective, assure him you're not arguing. You are under no obligation to do what he says. Thank him for his advice; then select those parts you can use. Use the judgment you do when eating fish; pick out the bones before you swallow anything.

Control in conflict begins with control of yourself. But good counsel can help you develop that self-control. "Listen to advice and accept instruction,/and in the end you will be wise" (Prov. 19:20, NIV).

Structure. Control begins within the person who *wants* to exercise it. The mind must design structures to channel thought forces that surge through it like a rushing river. Puritan theologians used to say, "Fore-fancy your death bed." In other words, think about how you will react to a crisis when it comes. Decide on your attitude and anticipate your behavior. Schools have disaster drills so the children will know what to do if a catastrophe strikes. We must make mental plans of how we will react to controversy.

The mental structure for control involves basic attitudes. These attitudes may be determined by asking ten questions in anticipation of controversy.

1. How will integrity and propriety control my behavior?
2. What values will dominate my decisions?
3. What are the roots of our disagreement?
4. What do I care most about in this dispute?
5. What resources will I need to pursue this controversy?
6. What can be negotiated?
7. What cannot be surrendered?
8. What image will I project?
9. What are the risks?
10. What are my alternatives?

These questions can erect structures for the mind that will buttress our thoughts and emotions. They'll help us control our fears, restrain our impulsive actions, and direct our energies. If we fail to think about our thought processes *before* conflict, we are move vulnerable to our fears and emotions.

I was reflecting with a friend on a dilemma at our church. We questioned what I would do if certain things happened. He asked about my resources, visible and invisible; he explored my values and limitations. "What would you do," he asked, "if your strongest supporter withdrew from this battle?"

"I'd walk alone," I answered. "My convictions and commitment to God in this matter would demand it." Setting up that mental structure helped me stay on track. My supporters stuck with me, but an unanswered fear did not distract me.

In addition to the inner structures of the mind, the church should erect external systems to direct the forces that flood it in conflict. One of these structures is a set of church bylaws. Bylaws govern members in implementing the purpose and policies of the congregation. These rules describe how the machinery of the church organization is to be assembled and operated. Bylaws constitute the "rules of the game."

Early in my ministry I led our church to adopt a set of bylaws. Many times these rules have kept us from squabbling on and on over petty procedures. At times I have chafed under those rules which seemed too restrictive. But over the years their value has been proven over and over again. Bylaws are not written to restrain good actions, but to make possible the smooth development of a positive ministry.

At times in controversy, when bridled by rules or procedures, some people complain, "Why can't we just live by the Bible instead of these man-made bylaws?" These remarks are usually manipulative ploys to avoid specific guidance in controversy. One asking that question certainly ignores Paul's command to the Corinthian church: "Let all things be done decently and in order" (1 Cor. 14:40). Paul's appeal came at the close of his writing about a spiritual activity where things got out of hand. So the apostle set down rules, even for those led of the Spirit. He wrote, in effect, "Keep these rules or don't speak in tongues in the church."

If we are to keep matters from becoming chaotic where differences divide people, we must have the structure and guidance of rules. To reassure church members who fear such bylaws, let me emphasize three things which bylaws are *not* meant to be.

Bylaws are not meant to deprive either pastor or people of their rights within the church. These rules consider the rights of all members in relation to their responsibilities. Bylaws define rights, responsibilities, and procedures for both pastor and members. It helps them understand their freedom in an orderly relationship. Good bylaws will curb an overly ambitious pastor. They'll prevent him from pushing through some pet program without giving the congregation proper opportunity to consider the matter. These rules can protect the church from becoming dominated by a pastor or some power bloc of members.

In addition, bylaws should *not* become instruments of power to any individual or groups within the church. They are designed as aids for responsible ministry. Responsibilities must be assigned in an orderly fashion, along with adequate authority to implement ministry. Otherwise, everybody's right becomes nobody's responsibility.

Finally, we should *not* expect bylaws to serve as a "cure-all" for all church problems. No set of rules can cover every situation. Activities described in the bylaws are carried out by fallible people. Without common sense, such laws are folly; without kindness, there will be fanaticism; without love, there will be only discord.

Along with bylaws, a church business meeting deserves a person of integrity as presiding officer. He should also know parliamentary procedure. *Roberts' Rules of Order* are generally accepted guides for the democratic process.

Several times our congregation was very emotional when we met for business. Strong personalities were determined to dominate the proceedings. During those times of intense emotions, I exercised my responsibility as moderator to define basic parliamentary rules. The congregation understood that those rules would guide us during our business proceedings. This was done *before* the motions were made and debate got under way. This set the tone for the meeting and indicated control by proper rules. Had this not been done at times, we might have had shameful disorder.

In addition to rules through bylaws and parliamentary procedure, roles in a church also lend structure to conflict. Little attention is given to this type of structure in most churches. A role is an assigned or expected activity repeatedly performed by a person. A pastor has many roles. He is assigned to preach, so he has the role of a preacher. He may also have the role of an administrator and another role as a personal counselor. He can have the role of program planner, financial leader, and evangelistic director.

Members of the church also serve in various roles. The role of an usher may be assigned to a person who serves as a Sunday School teacher.

Problems and conflicts often arise in a church over role expectations. Sometimes a member expects the pastor to perform a certain function that the pastor does not consider his job. Conflict is inevitable when role expectations are different.

Role conflicts of a pastor are many. Often he is personally confused about what he should be doing. His sense of divine call confuses him when he lacks a clear awareness of his gifts and limitations. He tries to be "all things to all people."

The role pressures that a pastor may feel within himself are compounded by the ambiguities in his office. He and the church need to write precise descriptions of his various tasks. Otherwise, members will have conflicting views of what duties the pastor should perform.

I knew one young man who requested a specific job description upon his call to a church as their pastor. The members of this young church were not experienced with the complexities of the pastor's office. There was considerable confusion among the pulpit committee when this request was made. "We believe you are God's servant," one member protested. "All you need to do is look in the Bible to find out what you should do."

This person didn't consider a possible misunderstanding by the pastor and people over many day-to-day questions. When would the pastor have a day off and did he get sick leave? What was his vacation time? Could he have time for continuing his education or attending denominational conventions? What were his responsibilities in supervising staff members, and what were his powers of appointment? What about the limitations of his authority and his relationship to committees? These and many other questions needed to be clearly answered *before* the pastor began his ministry in the church. Otherwise, role conflicts were sure to happen.

Beside clear definition for the pastor's role, members and officers of the church need their roles clearly described. What is the role of a deacon? That answer will vary in churches, so it needs to be defined. What authority does the Sunday School director have? What are the bounds of responsibility for different church committees?

Many hurt feelings can be avoided if people understand and function within their assigned roles. Membership in a church does not give a person the right to invade areas of responsibility specifically assigned to others. In our democratic society a person does not have the right to assume authority in various areas of government just because he is a taxpaying citizen. We need to be educated about what we should and should not do in our church roles.

The word *structure* conveys a feeling of rigidity. But flexibility is important to conflict control. Resilience of structure is possible without constantly changing the rules. An organization may keep a sympathetic and elastic nature by bringing new members into the group. Rigidity develops more often from inflexible people than from strong laws. A rotation system in the membership is one way to keep a group from becoming insensitive and unbending.

Besides the structure of rules and roles, another technique for controlling conflict is *goals*. These are positive forces in guiding us away from controversy toward a desired purpose. The church should have great, overarching purposes for ministry. These are the New

Testament ideals toward which we pray and work. An example is the command for us to disciple all nations. Such a purpose is ever beyond us, but it gives direction to our ministry. Goals are the steps we take toward those purposes to which God calls us. Unless we take planned, measurable steps, we wander without direction, unaware of how far we have come toward fulfilling God's purpose.

For goals to be effective, they must answer these familiar questions: What is to be done? Why? Who will do it? What will be needed to accomplish it? When will it be finished? How will we evaluate the competed task?

Such goals move us to accomplish great things. But goals also have an important function not usually noticed; they are a powerful influence in controlling conflict. Without goals churches are prone to petty bickering which sometimes evolves into fights. The frustration of not having specific tasks of ministry generates anger. This stirs dissension. Good goals are strong control structures within a church for several reasons.

Goals are clarifying lights on what we should be doing as servants of Christ. I met with a church council to plan for the future. We were fuzzy about what we should recommend to the church for the next few months. At the close of the meeting a new member of the council asked a penetrating question: "What we've been doing tonight—is this why we are here?" He asked this in genuine sincerity without a trace of criticism. Behind the question I could feel his frustration about whether there was something more significant we should be doing. The question haunted me. I resolved to lead the people into better planning with more significant goals.

We often make the mistake of equating activity with accomplishment. We get busy without achieving anything significant. Goals clarify our activities and call us back to the purpose of God for our lives.

With proper goals we have a structure that keeps us from squabbling over merely "doing something" and focuses our concerns on God's divine purpose for our lives. If we cannot see that we are moving closer to God's purpose by pursuing a goal, we should reexamine what we are doing. Proper goals focus on God's purpose for the church.

Goals are cohesive forces that draw the people into a close fellowship. The description of the disciples at Pentecost is a beautiful ideal for the church. "They were all with one accord in one place" (Acts 2:1). Harmony of spirit and unity of purpose can be experienced when people have a common goal. Many congregations have experienced strong togetherness like this when they suffered a tragedy such as a flood or a fire.

A better illustration of the cohesive force of a goal was experienced by our church one summer. We were in a state of apathy with some petty bickering. We were drifting into the summer without any unifying activity. A fellow pastor across town suggested that his church and ours have a Sunday School attendance contest. The losing church would host the winning church at an ice-cream feast, and the winning pastor would throw a pie in the face of the losing pastor. I thought it a bit trivial, but I had nothing better in mind for a long, dull summer. I also realized that his church was a bit larger than ours and was located in a fast-growing section of the city, but we accepted the challenge. Our people worked together with enthusiasm. I was amazed to hear some people whom I thought totally indifferent to Sunday School say, "Nobody's going to smack our preacher in the face with a pie!" The goal drew our people together in work and fellowship. And we won! Goals are a cohesive force.

Goals concentrate power by drawing energy and resources from people for great endeavors. Worthy goals challenge the best service people can render in the name of the Lord.

When our church was dying numerically and financially, we set a great goal. We determined to move our church from an effete area to a new location and build a dramatic new building. It was amazing how much was done by so few people. They gave sacrificially and worked tirelessly to reach that goal. And they did!

Goals are also a culminating instrument that aids the evaluation of our work. Goals must have a time limit and a measurement for what is to be accomplished. Goals force us to look at ourselves and what we are accomplishing. During conflicts we don't like to evaluate. In controversy we do a lot of judging but not evaluating. We judge the other fellow and justify ourselves when we are contentious. We seldom evaluate our own work during a quarrel. Goals remind us of a task and so control our tendency toward conflict.

If you want to get control of yourself or a group, set worthy goals.

To be in control, we must erect structures to control our thoughts and guide our behavior. Otherwise, emotions will run rampant, and our behavior will become irresponsible and destructive.

Strategy. Control in conflict comes from the spirit, through study and structure. But to be effective these agents of control must work together. Strategy is a plan for relating these resources to conflict.

Some people withdraw from the scene of conflict and so have nothing further to do with it. That is withdrawal strategy.

Spectator strategy is used by people who do not want to withdraw from the scene. They want to see what develops but refuse to help find a solution. These people give their opinions from the sidelines, but take no risks in the struggle.

Covert strategy is sometimes used by those insecure in their lives or insensitive to Christian integrity. Hidden plans are made to defeat the opposition without consulting facts or feelings.

I knew a pastor who presided over a very controversial matter when it was brought to a congregational vote. The ballots were counted, and "the motion passed" report was handed to the pastor. He read it to the congregation, and the meeting was dismissed. However, in all innocence, the teller committee that counted the votes had made a mistake.

In the days that followed, people who lost the vote searched for flaws and found the error. They did not go to the pastor about it; nor did they inquire of the teller committee. They covertly planned a public humiliation of the pastor by making accusations of dishonesty and conspiracy. This they set out to do at a Sunday morning worship hour. The pastor's professional career would have been devastated. Chaos would have errupted in the fellowship of a strong church.

In the providence of God, the pastor learned of the error, checked with the chairman of the teller committee, and told him a correction must be announced the next Sunday. When the pastor planned this correction, he was unaware of the secret strategy being developed by the opposition. He did make that announcement the Sunday morning following the business meeting, thus averting a tragedy. Covert strategy is not Christian behavior. Neither does it resolve controversy in the spirit of concern for the family of God.

The above types of strategy do not offer the solution to conflict which befits the church. Control by strategy is the careful planning of responsible people who seek the best solution for the whole church. This does not imply there will be unanimity throughout the congregation; but the welfare of the whole church will be sought.

The control of conflict by strategy is seldom used in a church for several reasons. The very presence of a controversy is considered as abnormal and bad. Therefore, conflict is ignored if at all possible. Disagreements make people ill at ease; few are willing to work out a plan to solve the problem.

In addition, we tend to personalize when we are in conflict. We focus on the person rather than the problem. Then we become emotional over personal factors totally unrelated to the disagreement.

Another reason churches avoid the use of strategy in conflict resolution is that it takes time. In church we are prone to shortcuts. Even our theology gives us heaven in a single step. Then why shouldn't everything else in church be as simple and easy? We are reluctant to give time to planning, especially when it concerns something unpleasant. We prefer to function impulsively rather than rationally.

If we would take time to decide ways of resolving our differences, we would save time. A serious conflict consumes a great deal of time. If many people are emotionally hurt there is also a long healing period lost from productive ministry. Time spent in thoughtful planning should involve at least three stages. The first step in managing any conflict is to define the problem. When the difficulty is clarified, some effort should be made to defuse the emotions of those affected by the tension. Then decide upon a course of action to resolve the conflict. Such strategy will be more likely to control feelings and get a desired response than an uncontrolled dispute.

Define the problem. There is an axiom that a problem precisely stated is half solved. When we understand the question well enough to state it clearly, we are on our way to a solution. Some controversies become so involved that people do not know what they are arguing about.

In planning a strategy for controlling a particular conflict, we should write down the problem so that all involved can see and agree on that statement. The simpler the statement, the better. What do we wish to accomplish through this struggle? If possible we should relate the problem-statement to a church goal. If the issue is not goal related, the dispute may be irrelevant. When opponents can agree on a particular problem, they have taken a step together.

Defuse emotions. Defensive emotions are barriers to reconciliation. Fear is a strong hindrance to peace. Sometimes I've started a personal reconciliation attempt with an adversary by saying, "You frighten me! I don't want to be afraid of you, but I am." The usual response to that is, "I'm afraid of you, too." Then we find ourselves on common ground.

Most church tensions have the element of fear in them. People are afraid they are going to lose some status before the church. They fear the loss of power or privilege. They are apprehensive of change. These fears make them defensive and motivate some to initiate an attack.

If those involved in conflict can be assured that their rights and points of view will be respected, tension can be eased. Anxiety and anger can be defused by reassuring the opposition of your concerned attitude. People are more sensitive to attitudes and feelings than to facts. Communicate with a sincere attitude and gentle words.

Slowing down the conflict process will often defuse emotions. When people know they will have time to deliberate, negotiate, and make a decision, they are less apprehensive. When the disagreement is turned into a shoot-out where the quickest and strongest wins, emotions flare. Slowing down the process cools tempers.

Defusing emotions can sometimes be done by giving our adversaries opportunity to talk it out. When we listen to people with genuine interest in their point of view, they are reassured and tensions ease. When persons can "blow off some steam" about their feelings, they often cool down and gain a better perspective of the problem.

These basics for church conflict apply to personal hostilities also. A friend of mine had been counseling a wife about some family problems. Her husband had been reluctant to talk with that pastor. When he finally talked with the preacher, he poured out an avalanche of anger. After some minutes of raging over his problems, he paused and spoke to the pastor with some amazement: "I didn't realize I was so terribly angry at my wife! I never have told her I felt like this." He smiled with embarrassment, thanked the pastor for listening, then went home and rebuilt his marriage.

Attentive listening often defuses harmful emotions. This easing process affirms a person's worth. It recognizes that person's need to have his self-esteem reinforced. It calms his fear that his values may be ignored.

Decide on a course of action and follow through. This is the final basic step to a strategy of conflict control. Fundamentals of problem solving must be used to decide upon a course of action. Certain questions help shape our plans.

What do we want to do? Three ways of resolving conflict while remaining in a good relationship are: reconciliation, negotiation, and mediation. In reconciliation the differing parties come together in mutual forgiveness and concern, so they can move in harmony toward a common goal. Through negotiation the people work together, each making compromises, to reach a mutually beneficial goal. By mediation, the differing parties agree to accept the decision and recommendations of a neutral referee. By this agreement they maintain their relationship and resolve the conflict through a mediator.

Who is to be involved in this work? Is a selected group to solve the problem? Is the entire congregation to be active in a meeting to resolve the disagreement? Such congregational debates, as a rule, are not productive. The congregation usually gathers in the sanctuary, which is not at all conducive to dialogue.

When will we schedule our meetings? The times must be reasonably convenient for the people involved.

Where will we convene? This question is often asked indifferently. In size and environment the place should fit the people who will be there. A small group in a large room or a big number in a crowded place affects the mood of the meeting. So does the lighting, the temperature, and ventilation. If you want the people alert and sensitive, keep the temperature lower than normal, without being cold. Too much heat slows down reactions and causes lethargy and irritability. Normal temperatures would seem best for most meetings. Well-ventilated rooms are a must for comfort and good disposition.

What resources will be needed? Prepare for supplies and resources to aid the meetings before the people arrive. That shows consideration for those attending. If the plan calls for research or travel, money for these expenses must be considered. All of these questions form the course of action in managing conflict.

Both in formal meetings and in informal contacts with people, one thing is extremely crucial: *our manner*. Manner is the *way* we do anything. It is the facial expression, the body language, the tone of voice. Manner is the feeling we communicate, the intensity or indifference of our attitude. People react to our manner before they hear our words. An ancient Scot proverb warns, "The manner is to the matter as the powder is to the ball." In other words, the *way* we say a thing determines the impact of our words. When the author of Proverbs wrote "A gentle answer turns away wrath,/but a harsh word stirs up anger" (15:1, NIV), he was teaching the importance of manner.

Summing Up. Conflict is inevitable between people who have any significant relationship. Differences of opinion are part of our being in this world. From the time of man's creation he has experienced conflict. God planted a controversial tree in Eden and permitted the contentious serpent within paradise. Here inevitable confrontation was thrust upon Adam and Eve. The forbidden tree became the focal point of their conflict with right and wrong. The striving with what we feel to be right or wrong still disturbs us. However, it is the struggle that develops our character and displays the grace of God to us, whatever the outcome of our conflict.

NOTES

CHAPTER 1

1. Saul Bellow, *To Jerusalem and Back* (New York: The Viking Press, 1976), p. 161.

CHAPTER 2

1. Paul Tournier, *The Meaning of Persons* (New York: Harper & Row, 1957), p. 38.

CHAPTER 3

1. Paul Tournier, *Guilt and Grace* (New York: Harper & Row, 1962), p. 75.
2. Edward B. Lindaman, *Thinking in the Future Tense* (Nashville: Broadman Press, 1978), p. 28.
3. Louis Brandeis, *Quote* (April 26, 1970), p. 386.
4. Elizabeth R. Skoglund, *To Anger with Love* (New York: Harper & Row, 1977), p. 17.

CHAPTER 4

1. Henry Fairlie, *The Seven Deadly Sins Today* (Washington, D.C.: New Republic Books, 1978), p. 37.
2. Ibid., p. 79.
3. Leslie H. Farber quoted by Elizabeth O'Connor, *Eighth Day of Creation* (Waco: Word Books, 1971), p. 40.

4. Abraham Zaleznik, *Human Dilemmas of Leadership* (New York: Harper & Row, 1966), p. 76.

CHAPTER 6

1. William Barclay, *The Gospel of John*, vol. 1 of *The Daily Study Bible Series*, rev. ed. (Philadelphia: The Westminster Press, 1975), p. 117.
2. Martin Buber, quoted by Kenneth O. Gangel, *Competent to Lead*, 2nd ed. (Chicago: Moody Press, 1976), p. 11.

CHAPTER 8

1. Thomas J. Watson, Jr., *A Business and Its Beliefs* (New York: McGraw-Hill, 1963), p. 3.

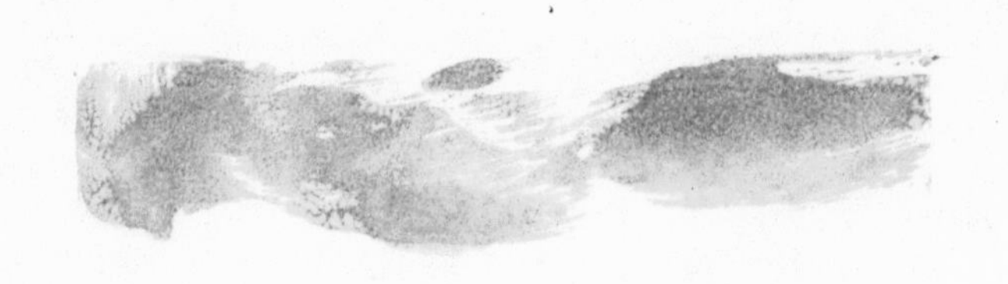